Legal Practice in the Digital Age

Legal Practice
in the
Digital Age

The quest for the killer legal app

CHARLES CHRISTIAN

SPONSORED BY SOLICITEC

BOWERDEAN
PUBLISHING COMPANY LIMITED

Published by The Bowerdean Publishing Company Ltd.
of 8 Abbotstone Road, London SW15 1QR

First published in 1998

British Library Cataloguing-in-Publication Data.
A catalogue record for this book is available from the British Library.

ISBN 0 906097 35 5

Printed by WBC Book Manufacturers, Bridgend, Mid-Glamorgan.

Contents

Foreword

Killer apps – "*In high-tech marketing, specifically in the PC industry, the killer application has enjoyed a status comparable to that of the Holy Grail. It is the application that drives forward an entire market.*"
GEOFFREY A. MOORE – CROSSING THE CHASM

Since the latter half of the 1970s, lawyers in just the UK alone have spent an estimated £2000 million between them on computerisation and similar law office automation projects.

Furthermore, with many law firms currently bringing forward their IT (information technology) projects in anticipation of possible Year 2000 computing problems (the so-called 'Millennium Bug'), it looks as if the current trading year (1998/99) will be the best yet with the total IT spend for the UK legal market likely to be in excess of £220 million.

Although these figures take into account not only hardware and software but also training and implementation plus ongoing annual maintenance and support costs, this is still an impressive figure. But what benefits have there been?

The answer, sadly, is not a lot. Indeed in most firms all this investment in IT boils down to little more than buying accounts and wordprocessing systems. Both of these merely replace older mechanical technologies – adding machines and typewriters – that performed exactly the same functions. Both are primarily 'back office' support systems to help cashiers, secretaries and clerical staff in their work and offer little or no tangible benefits to the lawyers in the 'front office'.

Or, to put it another way, over the past quarter of a century, lawyers have spent large amounts of money on IT systems that most of them can ill afford (apart from the acquisition of office premises, buying a new IT system is the single largest item of capital expenditure many law firms will ever make) and for no apparent purpose or benefit.

What lawyers have always wanted are systems that will help, or even transform, the way in which they carry out their legal work or 'lawyering' activities. But what they keep getting are systems that merely seem to make life easier for everyone else in the firm except the lawyers. In fact it is arguable that these systems actually make life more difficult for lawyers as they need to work harder to pay for them.

So where and why have lawyers been going wrong? Will there ever be such a thing as a 'killer app' (a software application that really does transform the user's working life) for the legal profession? And what impact, if any, will the new generation of 'digital' technologies (the Internet, the world wide web, the information superhighway, cyberspace *et al*) have on the legal world?

This book sets out to answer some of these questions and, in the process, reaches the conclusion that "yes" there are technologies out there that can benefit lawyers but unfortunately the legal profession has spent the last 25 years approaching IT from the wrong direction.

Charles Christian   **www.cloudnine.co.uk**
July 1998   **info@cloudnine.co.uk**

Chapter One

THE LEGAL WORLD IS NOT WHAT IT USED TO BE

"The first thing we do," says one of Shakespeare's revolting peasants in Henry VI, Part 2, "let's kill all the lawyers". No need to do that today, as a radically different commercial and professional environment is causing many practitioners to rue the day they ever set foot in a law school.

Before starting to consider the potential impact of new digital technologies on lawyers, we first need to consider some home truths about the current state of the legal world and look at the competing visions for the profession's future direction.

Speak to almost any lawyer today – well at least any lawyer practising within one of the major common law jurisdictions of the United Kingdom, North America, Australia, New Zealand or the Irish Republic (Eire has almost as high a ratio of lawyers to non-lawyers as Washington DC, which is currently the most densely legally populated place on earth) – and you will hear the same sad lament, namely that the life and times of the modern lawyer are not what they used to be.

Legal service at a premium

The overheads associated with the cost of running law firms are steadily going up. The one exception to this is the cost of professional indemnity insurance cover which, far from steadily increasing, is rocketing upwards in leaps and bounds.

For example, in England and Wales, which falls within the jurisdiction of the English Law Society (otherwise known as Chancery Lane) the cost of the mutual-based Solicitors' Indemnity Fund (SIF) has soared to a level where some lawyers are already having to abandon specific 'high risk' areas of practice because they cannot afford the SIF contributions.

In 1997/98 premiums were increased by an average of 50 percent and the fund still had a shortfall of £450 million. (This is nearly four times as much as the whole profession spends each year on IT.) Practitioners with major conveyancing and property related practices – 45 percent of all claims stem from property work – could face a 100 to 200 percent increase in their premiums.

The clients are revolting

Clients have become increasingly demanding in terms of the quality and speed of service they expect. They want the answers and they want them now. Unfortunately, they are also far more likely to query the bill and, should they not be 100 percent happy with the outcome of proceedings (and in the case of litigation, few clients are ever fully satisfied) they will sue for negligence or accuse the lawyer of unethical conduct and call for their professional body to instigate disciplinary proceedings.

Latest figures from the UK's Legal Services Ombudsman reveal that in 1997/98 there was a further seven percent increase in the total number of complaints being made against the 71,000 solicitors practising in England and Wales. The figure now stands at the equivalent of one complaint for every three solicitors. Ombudsman Ann Abraham said the rate at which complaints were being made was accelerating and that the Office for the Supervision of Solicitors was in danger of being 'overwhelmed' by the volume of complaints. All of which in turn, of course, helps bump up the cost of professional indemnity insurance cover.

Everyone wants a piece of the cake

Today's lawyers also face far greater competition – and not just from other law firms, although a relaxation on the rules governing advertising and promotional activities has inevitably made inter-firm rivalry more cut-throat than it ever was before.

Banks, financial institutions, insurance companies, estate agency chains and accountancy practices are all getting in on the act, offering services in the fields of trusts, tax and estate planning, probate, property sales, general business law advice, legal risks insurance and corporate restructuring – to name just a few areas that were once the sole preserve of lawyers. Indeed most of the UK's major accountancy practices, including Arthur Andersen, Price Waterhouse, KPMG and Ernst & Young, either have set up or are in the process of setting up their own legal networks through mergers with law firms.

As well as adding yet another downward pressure on the fee levels that can be charged, this greater competition is also forcing firms into a position where for many, their very survival depends on scrabbling around for low margin work, with a consequent significant increase in the number of billable hours that have to be worked each week if they are to make ends meet.

Lawyers are human too

Add together the pressures on profits and time, their poor reputation (rightly or wrongly) with the public in general (who hasn't heard an anti-lawyer joke?), politicians (criticising 'fat cat' lawyers never lost anyone votes) and, rather more importantly, their clients, and you can see why many lawyers now feel so sorry for themselves. Quite simply, their once envied quality of lifestyle has all but disappeared.

A partner in the now defunct City of London firm Turner Kenneth Brown told me that what really got him down was not the long hours, nor getting home just before midnight knowing the first meeting of the following day was scheduled for 8.00am, nor working most weekends, nor even having to come into the office on Christmas Day. What really got him down was knowing that the brand new Porsche 911 he had bought to celebrate being made a partner was now nearly three years old and sitting in his garage under a dust sheet with still less than 400 miles on the clock.

Furthermore, it is not just the members of larger law firms – where the scramble up the promotion ladder to full partnership has long been an unseemly dog-eat-dog scramble – who are under pressure. The senior partner of a small litigation practice in north London admitted she was so concerned she might overlook something relating to work that she never let her laptop computer leave her side. Never. It goes home with her for the evening. She takes it with her on holiday. She even has it running on stand-by next to her bed, in case she thinks of something and wakes up in a cold sweat in the middle of the night.

And, do not lose sight of the fact this decline in lifestyle is also dragging down with it many lawyers' personal lives. Long working hours do not make for happy families or stable relationships although they do provide plenty of opportunities for affairs.

Similarly, high stress levels and their associated palliatives – cigarettes, alcohol and recreational drugs – do nothing for a lawyer's health. The Washington State Bar in the United States reckons that 18 percent of lawyers have addiction problems of some kind. The English charity Solcare estimates that 10 percent of all 'City' lawyers have serious alcohol related problems.

What undoubtedly makes this state of affairs even less

palatable for today's lawyers – as they work late into the night pondering their failing marriages and wondering whether their first nervous breakdown will strike before or after their first coronary – is that most of them have been in practice long enough (or at least have colleagues who have been in practice long enough) to remember a time when life wasn't like this. And it was not all that long ago.

Halcyon daze

The period from the late 1940s, when the economies of the USA and Western Europe were recovering, through to the early 1980s can now be seen as a halcyon era for lawyers. True, hourly fee earning rates had not reached current heady heights, but with far lower overheads and virtually no competition, profit margins were healthier and business pressures much easier.

State of the art legal technology for much of this period was largely confined to telephones, visible record card accounting machines, Rolodex-style card index systems, typewriters and magnetic tape-based dictation machines.

Of course commercial success still depended on a combination of legal skills and hard work but there were far fewer dawn starts or late nights to disrupt the average partner's 10-til-5 routine. This was also the era of the long and leisurely business lunch, followed by an afternoon at the club or a round of golf with clients. There was still time for a social life, dinner parties or visits to the theatre – without the fear that at any moment your pager would summon you to an urgent meeting with clients.

There was also still time for plenty of holidays. The summer holiday period, technically termed the Long Vacation by lawyers, really was one long vacation. When I was in practice at the Bar, it was a standing joke that there were more barristers, solicitors and judges to be found in Tuscany and the Provence region of France during August than there were in the whole of London.

So what happened?

The short answer is that for a host of commercial, legal and political reasons, the legal community found itself rudely transformed almost overnight from being just another 'Ye Olde Worlde Profession', whose methods had changed little from the days of the early nineteenth century when Charles Dickens still worked as a court shorthand reporter, into a profit-motivated business that had to sink or swim in the booming financial environment of the 1980s.

Greed is good

It was the era of the Thatcherite monetarist revolution in the UK and Reaganite economics in the USA – a period when fictional character Gordon Gekko's dicta that 'greed is good' and 'lunch is for wimps' best summed up the prevailing business ethic. It was a time of 'Big Bang' in the London financial community. And big financial deals meant very big fees for the commercial law firms of Wall Street and the City of London.

It was a time when the old 'Perry Mason' television role model of the lawyer as the friend of the underdog, who was more concerned with justice than money, was replaced by the glitz of 'L.A. Law' (or 'This Life') where the lawyer screwed the underdog, sometimes both physically as well as metaphorically.

There were also a host of often minor changes that were to have major repercussions. Globally there has been an easing of the professional regulations governing advertising and other forms of promotion, so firms now not only compete against each other to win clients, but also to secure and keep the best lawyers and fee earners.

In the UK, one of the most far reaching developments was a relatively minor change in company law which removed the old restriction limiting the number of partners in a solicitors' practice to a maximum of 20 – a simple move which opened the floodgates to what became known as 'merger mania', with firms combining and consolidating to create ever-larger practices capable of competing on a regional, national, international or even global basis.

And the clients are becoming even more revolting

Unfortunately for the legal profession, these developments were not taking place in a vacuum. Just as the 1980s were a boom period that transformed the way lawyers ran their practices, conducted their business, treated their staff and viewed their clients, so the decade also witnessed a marked shift in attitude among all the other participants in the legal business.

We have already seen that clients are now more inclined to query the bills they receive from their lawyers than in previous decades, but this less deferential attitude towards lawyers is also reflected in other ways.

For example, regardless of whether they are actually happy with the skills and performance of their existing providers of legal services, it is now common practice for larger clients, particularly those with inhouse legal departments, such as major corporates, government bodies and financial institutions, periodically to review their legal advisers and require them to make competitive business presentations (otherwise known as 'beauty parades' – a concept previously only encountered within the advertising and public relations industries) to ensure they are getting the most commercially attractive deal.

This decline in client loyalty has also been echoed in the private client sector, once the bread-and-butter staple of High Street law firms, where the idea of the 'family lawyer' has given way to price and speed of service as the main criteria for selecting or retaining legal advisers.

In both private client and commercial practice it used

to be a fairly safe assumption that if you did a good job for the client today, they would automatically return to you in the future when they had more business. Now, only the wildly optimistic or sadly complacent make such assumptions. The rest are just grateful to be paid for the work they have done.

The last few years have also seen a profound change of priorities among the other people and organisations who regularly deal with lawyers on a professional basis. The result is that one-time friends, colleagues and confederates can no longer be seen as allies but must now be viewed as potentially hostile commercial competitors.

Accountants, bankers, insurance brokers, building societies and estate agents no longer automatically refer work to local independent law firms on a mutual back-scratching basis.

Instead, they handle it directly through their own inhouse legal departments. (Hambro Countrywide is setting up a national network of 'one stop' property shops offering everything from estate agency to mortgage provision and conveyancing services.) Or, as in the case of the big accountancy practices, they effectively buy their own law firm subsidiaries. Or, they just put the work out to commercial tender – the beauty parade again – and let old loyalties go to the wall.

Worse still, at least from the point of view of law firms, is that thanks to the reorganisation, re-engineering and centralisations within other institutions, one time reliable business partners have disappeared.

That friendly, always-approachable local bank manager you used to meet at golf club tournaments, masonic dinners and Rotary Club barbecues – and who would always grant a business loan or extend an overdraft facility in times of need – has been replaced by an impersonal, unapproachable regional manager who knows nothing of your practice's cash-flow idiosyncrasies and cares only about budget controls and personal guarantees.

Technology cuts both ways

By way of a further entry to our list of woes, it is also worth noting that one of the major items of expenditure on most law firms' shopping lists in recent years – their investment in new computer systems and other forms of office technology – has itself proved to be a double edged sword, solving some problems while at the same time creating fresh difficulties to be resolved.

For example, computer systems might automate some business processes but at the expense of having to employ additional staff, change existing procedures and embark upon an apparently endless cycle of system upgrades, enhancements and replacements.

Even such an apparently innocent (and useful) piece of equipment as a photocopier has led to so great an explosion in the volume of paperwork associated with all forms of legal practice (but litigation in particular) that we now need a whole new family of technology – including indexing, database and litigation support software, as well as full text retrieval, optical character recognition (OCR), document image processing (DIP) and electronic document management (EDM) systems – to keep pace with it.

A few years ago I interviewed Sir Henry Brooke in his capacity as a member of the Information Technology and the Courts (ITAC) civil litigation working party (he is now a judge in the English Court of Appeal and still very actively involved in championing the use of IT within the courts). He warned that "thanks to the curse of the photocopier" the courts system was in danger of being overwhelmed by paper. Too many lawyers, he felt, were already taking the view that, if in doubt, instead of worrying about the relevance of a particular document, just photocopy it and add it to the bundle the other side will later have to wade through during discovery, or counsel and the judge will have to cope with at the trial.

In the 1970s advocates could still carry the documents in the case (the more important ones flagged by 'Post-it' notes) to court with them each morning. Today, by comparison, with some mega-trials (particularly fraud cases, major contract disputes and group negligence actions) involving hundreds of thousands – if not millions – of documents, managing all this largely technology - generated paperwork has become a significant logistical task in its own right. It can only be tackled with the assistance of yet more computer technology (as well as a new breed of legal assistant – the litigation support para-legal), while getting the documents to court often requires the services of a removals firm armed with a pantechnicon.

With such dramatic changes sweeping through the legal community within the space of a little more than 15 years, the inevitable concern facing not just the current generation of lawyers but also their children – the next generation of lawyers – is what does the future hold in store for the profession?

Since the early 1980s we have moved from a legal 'profession' to a legal 'business'. But what comes next?

Will there be a return to 'the good old days'? Or, will we see a worsening of today's grim sweat shop tendency, with a move towards a legal 'industry' and an even greater deterioration in lifestyle? If so, it will surely drive out some of the legal world's best minds to pursue alternative careers. (In 1996 the partners in charge of the tax departments at two major London firms, Simmons & Simmons and Slaughter & May, both quit because of what one described as the "ridiculous hours" they were expected to work.)

Clearly the legal community is on the cusp. But in which direction is it now heading?

Chapter Two

COMPETING VISIONS OF THE LEGAL FUTURE

"But in this world nothing can be said to be certain, except death and taxes," said Benjamin Franklin and he was also one of the first people to observe we should "remember, that time is money". Both are sentiments lawyers can sympathise with. Today however, the profession also has other issues to consider.

If we draw together all the various strands now in circulation – the legal and technical developments of the last decade, current business and IT trends, the opinions advocated in the legal media and the hopes and aspirations expressed by lawyers engaged in legal profession 'politics' – three main trains of thought can be identified. Each offers its own competing vision of the future for the legal profession.

I have christened these: the Pre-Millennium Pessimists, the Millennium Optimists and the Post Millennium Realists.

PRE-MILLENNIUM PESSIMISTS

As might be expected, the Pre-Millennium Pessimists have the blackest view of the future. According to their scenario, present trends in law office automation, cost cutting and price competition will accelerate over the next couple of years.

For smaller firms, survival will depend on the sausage machine model – in other words the ability to process greater and greater volumes of increasingly lower paid work (the Legal Aid Practitioners Group already reckons that some lawyers are earning an average of a mere £10 an hour). This in turn means even longer hours, more stress and a further erosion of client loyalty, all the while accompanied by an ever declining quality of life.

Bigger firms will still enjoy well-paid big ticket work, but there too lawyers will find their work becoming increasingly depersonalised and subject to the tyranny of billable hours targets. These are targets made all the more rigid by on-screen time recording systems and practice management software which can not only account for, but also analyse in great detail every second of the lawyer's working day.

Or, as the joke goes: the law firm of the future will have three components – a computer, a lawyer and a dog. The computer is there to do the work. The dog is there to keep the lawyer away from the computer and the lawyer's job is to feed the dog. Sounds grim? It is and its impact is already starting to be felt.

According to one recent survey, nearly 40 percent of all trainee solicitors would like to quit the profession and are only hanging on because they have spent six or seven years training and qualifying for the job and have a pile of debts to pay off. One trainee even calculated she had earned more money as a student, when she had a summer job washing dishes in a hospital kitchen.

Another survey found that over a quarter of qualified lawyers were unhappy with their status in society. Over one-third said their earnings had not lived up to their expectations. A recent Law Society of Scotland survey found that 25 percent of sole practitioners were making a net profit of less than £16,000 a year despite, in some cases, working in excess of 65 hours a week. Over

50 percent of lawyers working in larger firms said the impact of legal work on their social life had been far worse than expected.

In the circumstances, perhaps what is surprising is not that 12 percent of the sample thought they would be following a career outside of law in the year 2002, but that 88 percent thought they would still be practising law. (Of those opting out of the rat race because they do not wish to become the legal equivalent of hamburger flippers in fast food restaurants, the most popular alternative careers were teaching, being an artist, writing, or being a stand-up comedian.)

Whenever I raise the topic of the lawyer's quality of life with the more senior partners of large firms, I never cease to be amazed by their apparent complacency and arrogance. The attitude seems to be: "If we pay people enough money, they'll put up with whatever we throw at them by way of unreasonable working hours and conditions". If you are happy to have a firm full of money-oriented *apparatchiks* then that is fine. But these firms risk the longer term haemorrhaging away of their brighter more dynamic brains.

MILLENNIUM OPTIMISTS

Turning to the Millennium Optimists, far from one single cohesive group, here we encounter a motley mixture of idealists and dreamers as well as the cheerfully oblivious and sadly deluded. In fact there are at least six different, although sometimes overlapping, strains of thought circulating among the legal profession's optimists...

Turn back the clock

There are the 'turn back the clock' brigade, who would like (and piously hope) to reimpose all the protectionist measures that have gradually been shed (or prised away from the legal profession) since the early 1980s.

Such a move would allow lawyers to enjoy their local closed shop monopolies once more. (The two most obvious examples are conveyancing and direct access in the case of English solicitors and rights of audience in the case of barristers. At the time of writing Lord Chancellor Irvine has just announced a further assault on the Bar's virtual monopoly on rights of audience in higher courts.) They could ring fence areas of legal work from fair and open competition by the likes of the banks and financial institutions, and enforce rigid price controls at the expense of clients, so inefficient firms are no longer undercut by competitors able to offer lower fee rates.

I suspect a lot of these backwoods lawyers are also upset by the change in the public's attitude towards the profession. Once clients were deferential, but now they have little loyalty and a far greater propensity to complain. This is something that not only was almost unheard of 15 years ago but was also very difficult without the disgruntled client being put to more expense.

In an embarrassing near-Freudian slip, made while posting a message onto an online legal bulletin board, one would-be legal profession politician made the following comment: "It's time for solicitors to start hitting back instead of meekly taking everything that is thrown at us. I will be more inclined to court the public when the public show that they deserve our respect by being perpared (*sic*) to pay a reasonable fee for our services."

Presumably this lawyer would also like members of the public to doff their hats and step to one side when he meets them in the street.

Sorry, these are pipe dreams. We live in a consumerist society now and no one is ever going to turn the clock that far back. Besides no political party of any persuasion has ever won (or is ever likely to win) votes on a platform of making it easier for lawyers to make money. Indeed, the competition policies now prevalent within the European Union suggest that the next 15 years will see a further erosion of trade barriers, so that in the future lawyers are likely to face even greater competition from outside agencies and other non-lawyers offering legal services to the public.

Firms fail in the sunset

Then there are the sunset firms, populated by lawyers who have their heads wedged firmly in the sand. The world may be fast changing around them, but they remain fixed in the postage stamps and fountain pens era of the 1950s. Sadly, I suspect this group is beyond help – or hope – and will see their firms close when their current principals and senior partners leave active practice.

These are the people who write to me saying they are not going to invest in technology because they "believe computers are a passing phase". Like the Teletubbies or Spice Girls I suppose. They also believe marketing and similar modern commercial practices are heresies that have no place in the legal world. Or, as one senior partner told me: "We tried marketing once but it didn't work".

There again, another told me the main reason he opted for a career in law was because it was a profession and that "if he had wanted to run a business, he would have gone into commerce instead". Perhaps the noteworthy feature about sunset firms is not that they are now going out of business but that they have managed to survive for so long.

Nevertheless it causes a lump in the throat to think that when a High Street law firm finally closes its doors, after conscientiously serving the local community for perhaps 40 years, its most valuable asset will not be its accumulated legal expertise and know-how or the practice's work in progress, but the redevelopment potential of its office building and car park space.

Business process re-engineers

Then there are the business process re-engineers who believe the way ahead lies through the reorganisation and restructuring of law firm management and internal operating procedures.

Such firms give the impression of being hives of activity. They have intricate sub-committee structures and go in for wide-scale recruitment of finance, IT and marketing directors from the commercial world and lawyers rejoicing in the zippy title of 'chief executive' rather than staid old 'managing partner'. Unfortunately all too often these changes amount to little more than tinkering with the existing system and lack any real substance.

Scratch the veneer and beneath the surface lie the same old back-stabbing internal politics, petty rivalries and demarcation disputes that have always dogged partnerships – a tendency flagged by the equally wide-scale movement of finance, IT and marketing directors back into the commercial world after, in some instances, only being able to stomach a few weeks of working for lawyers.

There is a very real danger that in the midst of all this pseudo-corporate re-engineering, drawing up mission statements (how can lawyers do this and still keep a straight face?) and approving designs for corporate logos, firms are actually losing sight of the real problems they face. Cynics might characterise this as the commercial equivalent of reorganising the deck chairs on the good ship Titanic.

But is there a market in the niche?
Then there are the advocates of specialisation, with law firms concentrating on one or more relatively narrow specialist areas of law. Instead of being generalists – the norm for most firms in the past – lawyers are now advised to become specialists, turning their practices into 'niche boutiques'. In fact the title of a paper delivered at one recent English Law Society conference was *Get a Speciality or Get Out.*

The specialisation route has its attractions – not least because it can and clearly does work for some practices. There have always been lawyers and law firms enjoying a healthy living from serving the needs of narrow niche markets as specialist practices and it makes sound business sense to focus on a few core areas rather than be a jack-of-all-trades. (Almost all barristers' chambers also pursue a degree of specialisation, with the barristers in those chambers in turn developing even narrower specialisms.)

But this is not a universal option and, if anything, suffers from the grave weakness of reflecting a metro-centric view of the legal world. True, the bigger legal centres of the globe – such as the City of London or Wall Street – can attract such a concentration of clients and work, some with almost unique requirements, that there is a sustainable demand for firms operating in often highly rarefied areas of legal practice.

Once you step outside these legal metropolises, the need for specialism fast evaporates. For the average lawyer working in the average UK High Street (or main street USA) law firm, there is simply not the volume of work to support a specialist practice. With a few exceptions, the catchment area for prospective clients is the immediate geographic area, with commercial survival depending on your ability to handle all and any work coming through your front door. (The unfortunate corollary is that some firms are so desperate for business that they accept work outside their field of competence and then get hit with a negligence claim, which in turn puts up professional indemnity premiums.)

Lawyers thinking of following the speciality route would do well to remember the old marketing adage: there may be a niche in the market, but is there a market in that niche?

Waiting for Godot

Next we come to the members of the Vladimir and Estragon tendency – those lawyers who, like the characters in the Samuel Beckett play, never do anything themselves because they are waiting for Godot to turn up.

In recent years the English legal world's Godots have taken many forms. These include attempts to promote or obstruct legislation going through Parliament, campaigns lobbying for increases in legal funding and a seemingly endless stream of committees of inquiry into the structure and operation of the legal profession and the provision of legal services.

In England, Lord Woolf's report *Access to Justice* (which contains excellent ideas but has yet to be backed by the necessary public funding to transform it from theory to reality) is the latest to find itself gathering dust on a bookshelf. Even relatively small-scale initiatives such as the English Law Society's 'High Street Starter Kit' (HSSK) project – a well-meaning but ultimately doomed attempt to source low cost computer systems for smaller firms, have been seized upon by lawyers hoping someone else was going to solve their problems for them.

(Actually we should not be surprised that some of these 'official' initiatives fail. The people behind the likes of the Law Society and the Bar Council are legal 'politicians' and bureaucrats, not IT visionaries. Or, as Sir Henry Brooke, who was mentioned earlier, commented in a recent speech, "I am bound to say that I have been rather disappointed by the absence of any very obvious strategic vision in these matters within the governing bodies of the Bar and the Law Society".)

Currently the new Godot on the block is the attempt by the English Law Society and others to promote the concept of 'solicitors' property centres' (or SPCs), where members of the public will be able to select properties and obtain all the legal and financial services associated with home buying from one source. This is an attempt by solicitors to compete with the 'all under one roof' operations now being offered by some of the larger estate agency/financial services chains, such as the Hambro Countrywide service mentioned earlier.

At the time of writing it is too early to judge whether

SPCs will be a success. They have worked in Scotland, but there again that country's property market has a different structure. As with all the other Godot projects that have come and gone before, they have been latched onto by the more desperate – and less imaginative – members of the legal profession as a potential universal panacea to all their problems.

Instead of facing up to reality and taking the initiative to resolve their own practices' problems (low profit margins, high overheads, administrative inefficiency, inability to recruit new fee earners, ageing client base, inadequate marketing, failure to win or keep new business) these lawyers are ducking the issues and hoping someone – or something – else will fix matters for them.

For instance, at the time of the HSSK project, large numbers of small firms that needed to and should have then been investing in new IT systems, simply stopped bothering even to look at the very wide range of products commercially available, because they were waiting, like Vladimir and Estragon, for the High Street Starter Kit to come along. The net result was that when the project failed, these firms were still in need of computerisation, only now they were also two years further behind those of their competitors who had already invested in IT.

It is, incidentally, one of the unwritten rules of computing that in terms of hardware, software and/or prices, there is never a 'right time' to buy IT. The ultimate deciding factor must be 'need'. You invest in IT when your business needs demand it. Wait too long for the perfect computer system (or Godot) to come along and you risk missing commercial opportunities, which could in turn jeopardise your practice's longer term prospects.

Paradigm lost
Finally, there are those who subscribe to the theory that we are about to witness the evolution of a 'new legal paradigm' and who believe that a change in the whole legal process, including the role

of the courts and the way lawyers provide legal services, will open up a so far untapped 'latent legal market'.

In the UK, the leading advocate of the new legal paradigm concept is Professor Richard Susskind, whose views are spelled out in his 1996 book *The Future of Law*. It is a fascinating book, but unfortunately – rather like Professor Stephen Hawking's *A Brief History of Time* – it appears to be one that few people have read from cover to cover and fully understood!

At its heart is the beguiling argument that a great many people do not use conventional legal services (in other words consult lawyers) because the whole process is so user-hostile, complicated, expensive or otherwise unattractive that these people are alienated from the law. But, says the good professor, if the law were packaged in a different way, so that it was accessible to everyone, in other words the latent legal market, more people would use it than do today.

Clearly this would be 'a good thing' as it is obviously desirable that warring neighbours should hurl injunctions at each other rather than bricks, bottles and abuse. Nevertheless, great though this may be for Joe Public and the creation of a more legally aware society, from the point of view of lawyers the concept would appear to have at least two serious flaws.

The first is whether there really is such a thing as a latent market of unsatisfied demand for legal services – or is law only ever going to be a topic of marginal concern to the population at large?

Will making the law more accessible really lead to millions of people waking up one morning, smacking themselves on the forehead and saying "Golly, gosh, today I really must apply for leave to start judicial review proceedings against my local authority because I believe they are acting *ultra vires*".

I think not. Apart from three exceptional situations, quite simply most people are law abiding citizens who manage to live their lives without ever having to come into contact with the law, the justice system or lawyers.

The three exceptions are: changing house (conveyancing), changing spouse (divorce) and death (wills and probate). However, there is already no shortage of both conventional legal assistance, via solicitors and alternative sources of legal advice. Citizens' advice bureaux, community law centres, banks, estate agencies and insurance companies (many of these now also offer legal advice telephone helplines as part of their service) all offer legal advice or D-I-Y guides on these subjects.

The fact is that the law is like dentistry. Although we all know we should look after our teeth and that the prevention of tooth decay is better than a filling or dentures, few people voluntarily set foot in a dentist's surgery. Instead they leave it until the last possible minute when the pain of toothache finally overcomes their fear of the drill.

Yes, more people should resort to the law to protect their legitimate rights and to resolve their disputes and if they did, there is no doubt many minor misunderstandings could be prevented from escalating into major disputes. But, just as no amount of dental education will ever instill greater enthusiasm for visiting the dentist, so no well-intentioned talk about the new legal paradigm will ever unlock a latent mass market for legal services.

Show me the money

A rather more fundamental and practical problem from the point of view of lawyers is, how will unlocking the latent legal market benefit the profession?

One of Richard Susskind's suggestions is that a great deal of valuable legal information and advice could be made accessible to a wider audience by making it available via the world wide web. Sounds a good idea, not least because there is a sizeable section of the community that is more familiar with surfing the

Internet for information than visiting their local library (if there is a local library) to try to locate the same material in a book.

And, with the British Government, Parliament and the Courts now making large volumes of legal-type information, including legislation and case reports, freely available via official web sites, this approach also has the added attraction of being far cheaper than buying copies of books, Acts of Parliament and law reports from bookshops and stationers.

But while it is one thing to create a people's law, it is an entirely different matter for lawyers to make money out of it. Or, as Susskind puts it: "the law is no more there to keep lawyers in business than ill health is there to provide a livelihood for doctors".

His view is that as more and more legal information becomes freely available via non-traditional mechanisms, such as the Internet, the demand for conventionally delivered legal services (via solicitors and barristers) will actually diminish.

It is hard to fault the logic of this. After all who is going to want to pay a lawyer for legal advice when they can get that same information free from alternative sources? However, this has not stopped a number of law firms from jumping on the new legal paradigm bandwagon, spending large amounts of money creating web sites, packing them full of useful free legal advice and then complaining that they have not generated any new business leads.

Possibly the one consolation for lawyers is that most of the people who make up the latent legal market – if it actually exists – would never normally use conventional legal services in the first place and so remain largely commercially irrelevant to the majority of the legal profession.

POST MILLENNIUM REALISM

There is, however, a third way, what this book calls Post Millennium Realism. This recognises that the commercial realities of the current legal business world are here to stay and that no amount of wishful thinking or trying to turn back the clock will ever restore the halcyon days of the 1950s, 60s and 70s.

It also accepts that a lawyer's life is likely to become, in the words of Thomas Hobbes, increasingly "solitary, poor, nasty, brutish and short", as competition – from both within the legal profession and from alternative legal service providers, such as banks and accountants – increases, with the result that there are more and more people chasing a slice of an already inadequate cake.

The Post Millennium Realist view also recognises that wo live in a world where the all-pervading influences of computing and communications technologies are inescapable facts of life. It believes that, rather than ignore IT, lawyers should try to harness it to their maximum advantage, as a way of both delivering legal services to an increasingly sophisticated client base and allowing practitioners to regain control of their workloads and start to recover some of that lost quality of life through increased efficiency, productivity and profitability.

The term I use to describe this techno-oriented approach is 'legistics' (meaning the use of advanced technologies to deliver legal advice and information services to clients and other lawyers) and its potentially greatest use is as a way of helping lawyers perform 'value added' legal work.

Value added? Ask a lawyer what they do for a living and they will usually say something along the lines of "we solve our clients' problems", "we provide legal advice" or "we interpret and apply the law to resolve disputes". Wrong. That may be what lawyers should be doing because that is what they have been trained to do and what their clients are happy to pay for. (And pay them they do – anything from £100 to £300 an hour and considerably more in the case of a conference with a top flight QC specialising in commercial law.)

But what they actually spend a considerable part of the

day doing – anywhere between 20 and 60 percent of the average working day – is shuffling bits of paper about and exchanging routine correspondence and telephone calls with clients about clerical matters.

Consider this scenario: you have a one hour meeting with the client at 10.00am, so you spend half an hour before the meeting locating the relevant files, reviewing the contents and preparing for the meeting. After the meeting you spend yet more time preparing file notes relating to the meeting and confirming any instructions arising out of that meeting with both the client and any other relevant parties. Then you have to file the papers away and begin the whole process all over again for your next appointment.

Even a brief telephone inquiry from a client can create a disproportionate amount of background clerical work – as well as interrupting and distracting you from the task in hand – compared with the actual legal advice element.

So what would you rather do? Spend eight hours working in the office doing value added legal work for which you can charge your highest hourly rate? Or spend eight hours working in the office, but only bill for a proportion of this time at full rate because the rest of the day has been taken up with administrative chores?

A client may be willing to pay £150 an hour to hear your legal advice but not for your services as a filing clerk. Admittedly it is accepted practice (even for Legal Aid work) to have a sliding scale of charge-out rates for different types of work so you can at least earn something for non-value added activities, such as dealing with telephone inquiries. But that is not a lot of consolation for a lawyer with high overheads and an overdraft to cover.

More to the point, if you are working on the basis of an agreed fixed fee for a job, as is now commonplace for much High

Street/private client work such as residential conveyancing, then every unbudgeted-for interruption by clients will seriously bite into your profit margin.

Legal technology systems (the application of legistics) can, should and must be harnessed to take over some or all of these functions so that lawyers and other fee earners can maximise the time they devote to value added work.

Chapter Three

EXCUSE ME, BUT HAVEN'T WE HEARD ALL THIS BEFORE ?

Taking time off from his opiates, Samuel Taylor Coleridge once wrote: "If men could learn from history, what lessons it might teach us!" Maybe – but apparently not in the world of legal technology.

Using technology to meet the needs of clients and maximise the efficiency, productivity and profitability of lawyers? But haven't we heard this before? In fact haven't legal systems suppliers and sundry IT consultants been selling us a version of the 'computerise or die' message for almost 25 years?

And, wait a minute. Isn't there a comment at the beginning of this book to the effect that lawyers have spent the last quarter of a century buying IT systems but have so far seen little or no tangible benefits, despite the vast amounts of money they have spent?

The answer to all these questions is "yes". But why hasn't technology been able to deliver the goods in the past? And why should we expect anything better in the future?

A useful starting point is to consider the supposed benefits of IT and some of the technologies that over the years have been advocated as being 'the next big thing' in law office automation.

As has already been mentioned, the first legal market-specific IT systems were almost exclusively confined to the 'back office'. There were accounts systems which, despite being fundamental to the successful operation of any business, in most legal practices only ever touched the working lives of cashiers and accounts department staff. And there were wordprocessors, firstly of the dedicated hardware variety and later PC-based, to replace typewriters. But, the only people to benefit were typists and secretaries – more back office staff.

Now, while such developments are admirable in their own way and are clearly going to produce some improvements in productivity and efficiency, in most law firms this means only about 50 to 60 percent of the total staff are using IT, leaving the other half – almost exclusively the lawyers and other fee earners within the practice 'front office' – virtually untouched by technology.

It was this scenario that fuelled the legal IT industry's ongoing quest for the Holy Grail of law office automation – the killer app that could simultaneously reduce overheads, increase productivity, boost efficiency, maximise profitability and generally transform the lives of lawyers. It would be the ideal application that would 'put a computer on the desktop of every fee earner' in the land.

The net result has been that over the years, lawyers have regularly found themselves being invited to conferences, exhibitions and supplier presentations at which a motley collection of offerings have each, in turn, been mooted as the proverbial next best thing since sliced bread.

Access all accounts

The first candidate for the title of legal industry killer app – and this takes us back to the early 1980s – was the suggestion that lawyers should have their own computer terminals linked to the back office accounts system 'to give them better access to management information'.

The theory here was (and in fact this concept is still being advocated today) that because law office computer systems contain a lot of potentially valuable information about clients and work-in-progress, instead of keeping this information locked up in the accounts department, it would be useful to make it accessible to fee earners via the PC or terminal on their desktops.

So, ran the theory, if you have Client 'X' coming in at 3.00pm to discuss some additional projects he wants you to handle, before he arrives you can call up his records to check not only what sort of work you have previously handled for him, but also if he pays his bills on time and how much unbilled work-in-progress is currently outstanding.

This makes commercial sense, as clearly you do not want to be taking on more work for a client who looks like being awkward about paying your fees for the work you have already carried out for him. No point in throwing away more good money after bad. But, do you need a computer system to tell you this?

For example, even assuming you can lay your hands on those always-easy-to-remember multiple character, alpha-numeric client and/or matter reference codes to locate the relevant files, are you confident you know your way sufficiently well around a solicitors' accounts software system, with its two-tier approach of separate client and office ledgers, to find specific items of financial information, let alone trying to run a new inquiry or search routine on a database retrieval system?

In the case of most lawyers the answer is "no" – which is why law firms employ accountants and cashiers to look after their bookkeeping. And in fact in most cases it is also a lot simpler, quicker and more convenient to phone the accounts department (or to get your secretary to do the job) and ask them to supply the background information about the client.

Anecdotal evidence suggests that this information is most frequently supplied by the accounts department in the form of a brief memo written on a Post-it note, which is then stuck to the VDU screen of the inquiring lawyer's computer terminal. Well it is nice to know all that investment in IT is not going entirely to waste!

The moving hand writes and having writ

Next came the suggestion that lawyers should do their own wordprocessing. Once again this is a suggestion which on first inspection appears to have merit. After all, the preparation of correspondence and legal documents is one of the most obvious products in any legal organisation and it this can be achieved without the expense of employing a secretary, surely it is going to help cut overheads and improve the bottom line?

Merely entering raw text has always been relatively easy with screen-based wordprocessing systems. The problem is actually putting that text into the correct layout and format so it can be printed off as a suitably professional document you can be proud to send to a client. Equally important is ensuring that the document is properly indexed and archived so it can be easily located at a later date – a far more time consuming activity.

The 'should lawyers do their own wordprocessing?' argument then boils down to a simple mathematical equation. Does it make more sense to have a lawyer, who could be earning £100, £200 or even £300 an hour, spending 45 minutes fiddling with the margins and line-spacing of a letter they are trying to print out? Or, would it be better to leave the job to a secretary, costing £5, £10 or £15 an hour to employ, who can do the job in five minutes?

This is not to say that lawyers should avoid all contact with wordprocessors. Clearly some familiarity with the technology is going to be useful for those occasions when the lawyer is working late into the evening or from home and does not have access to a secretary.

Similarly, lawyers just starting out in practice who can

neither afford nor have the volume of work to justify employing a secretary, also have a strong incentive to make the effort to master wordprocessing, as do those practitioners involved in cost sensitive areas of work – such as criminal legal aid cases and cut price conveyancing – where profit margins are already under pressure. (In fact some of the judges working out on the court circuits – where secretarial support services are minimal or non-existent – and barristers, who have always tended to be self-reliant when it comes to support services, are among the most skilled legal users of wordprocessing software.)

Nevertheless, while there may be some scope for lawyers doing their own wordprocessing, it needs to be kept in check if it is not to turn lawyers into the world's most highly paid secretaries.

The truth is out there

Another of the legal world's great new ideas was the online legal information retrieval system, also known as computer assisted legal research or CALR. (Lexis-Nexis and Westlaw are the two biggest players today.)

Apart from being launched prematurely, in fact about 15 years before the use of computers within the legal profession had reached a suitable critical mass to justify the enormous amounts of money suppliers were investing in the development of CALR systems, these products were based on a false premise.

The false premise here was what lawyers actually do with their time. I've already mentioned that shuffling bits of paper around takes up a lot of their day, but the politically correct answer is: they practice law. From this assumption, the logical conclusion might appear to be that 'law' is the key raw material for lawyers – in the same way that fresh peas are the key raw material for frozen pea processors such as Birds Eye.

It therefore follows that anything that can deliver law

to lawyers in a more convenient, speedy or otherwise efficient manner – and what could be better than an online system? – must be a good thing, as well as a sure fire recipe for financial success.

Tell that to the people in the UK who backed Eurolex, Infolex, BT's Network for Law, the National Law Library and, the most recent casualty, Law City. All were launched amid great hype but subsequently foundered – in some cases within months – for lack of users, enthusiasm and commercial prospects. (The experience of the online legal information services industry in the United States has been equally chequered.)

What went wrong? No one wanted their services, that's what went wrong. The simple – if unpalatable – answer is that once lawyers have qualified, the law in its purest form ceases to play an important role in their day-to-day legal practice. For example, for solicitors in High Street practice, the vast majority of conveyancing matters and matrimonial cases follow the same standard principles – a case of learn the law once and apply it many times.

Even in the more contentious aspects of legal practice such as criminal work and civil litigation, most cases merely revolve around applying familiar sets of legal principles (be it legislation or case precedents) to different sets of facts. When it comes to proceedings within the courtroom itself – and only a very small proportion of cases ever make it into court – it is still rare to encounter advocates arguing points of law. Instead, to use media-speak, their main role is to put the most positive (or negative) 'spin' possible on the facts at their disposal.

(I know one criminal barrister whose whole highly successful career has been built solely on his ability to stare prosecution witnesses straight in the eye and say, repeatedly: "I put it to you that you are lying". Works every time.)

The fact is that most lawyers are involved in a business that largely revolves around applying well established principles to new sets of circumstances and for that you do not need online legal information. Commonsense and intuition are far more valuable resources.

I should also add that on one occasion I raised this same argument in a magazine article and was promptly threatened with a libel writ by the director of a company providing CALR services. In the event, before he could take out a writ, his company was taken over and closed down by a rival. He lost his job and now sells furniture. *Res ipsa loquitur* – the thing speaks for itself.

The case is still undecided

Then there is the still ongoing saga of the case management system.

These first appeared in the late 1970s and early 1980s offering the promise of automating some areas of legal work such as debt collection processing. Instead of having endlessly to repeat the same procedures time and time again for each matter or client, the lawyer could be freed to concentrate on more complicated (and better paying) projects, while delegating the routine day-to-day aspects of the work to more junior (and lower paid) members of staff. The added bonus here was the 'management' element of the system still left the lawyer in overall control, while the operator (or 'non-cerebral fee earners' as one senior partner once rather cruelly described them) was guided through the task by the computer.

Well at least that was the idea. Unfortunately most of the early systems were highly inflexible in their design and more than a little idiosyncratic in the way they operated, thus presenting potential users with the less-than-attractive choice of either having to pay yet more money to have the software extensively customised, or else having to alter the way the firm traditionally handled that type of work so as to fit in with the way the software wanted to process it.

Although it is now widely accepted that any form of office automation must involve a degree of business process re-engineering (BPR) if users are to obtain the maximum benefit, with these early systems it was not so much a case of accommodating change as of the tail wagging the dog.

The widespread optimism which frequently greeted the introduction of these products rapidly faded when it became apparent that even these case management and similar so-called 'fee earner support' systems did not really lighten the load of the lawyer. Many of the tasks they were designed to perform were already being delegated to non-lawyer fee earners, such as secretaries, legal executives and what are now generally termed paralegals.

A further complication is that some firms also found that if they misjudged the respective roles of the lawyer and the paralegal, instead of effectively transforming junior staff into low paid fee earners, they were in danger of turning lawyers into highly paid paralegals – and the legal world's equivalent of hamburger flippers.

We are now hearing the praises of a new variation of this technology called the 'case management lite' system (in effect an automatic work scheduler plus diary and document management minder). In terms of hands-on benefits, this is yet another product which, although originally designed to help lawyers, is actually turning out to be of greater use to the non-lawyers within legal practices.

Greater productivity yes, but again not for lawyers.

Haven ice day

Another 'great white hope' – and one that has been the subject of tremendous publicity and hype in recent years – is speech recognition software.

Bearing in mind that the *modus operandi* of many lawyers is to dictate all their correspondence and file notes for subsequent transcription and typing up on a wordprocessor by a secretary, what could be better than a system that allows the lawyer to dictate directly into the wordprocessor?

In theory another good idea, as it builds on lawyers' already existing work methods (dictation), it offers an improvement in efficiency (no more time wasted correcting and amending the secretary's drafts) and it could lead to a reduction in overheads (the secretary can be sacked).

The reality is rather different. For example, you cannot dictate into a speech recognition system in the same way that you dictate to a secretary. A secretary is human and can understand out-of-context comments and asides. The computer on the other hand will just laboriously try to interpret your words and insert them in the text. These systems also need a lot of effort putting into them – hours, if not days – to get acceptable recognition speeds and accuracy levels. You also need very substantial PC hardware. And, if you are a computer 'phobe' who does not want to work with a keyboard, hard luck! You still have to master the computer to make these systems sing.

Perhaps the most telling comment on speech recognition software came at a recent 'Information Systems for Lawyers' conference. The speaker asked the delegates how many had tried speech recognition software – all put their hands in the air. He then asked how many were still using it – all put their hands down.

Undoubtedly speech recognition systems will overcome their problems, so that one day the microphone will be as familiar an accessory of the personal computer as are the mouse and keyboard today. But not just yet. In the meantime, the experience of most law firms remains that speech recognition systems are gadgets that soon lose their novelty value and get put back in the toy cupboard.

Fear and loathing in the virtual law office

Another concept that at one time had its advocates was telecommuting (or teleworking). Why come into the office when, thanks to laptop computers, email and video conferencing links, ISDN lines, communications networks and document management/file transfer systems, you can work just as conveniently from your home in the Cotswolds – or apartment in Provence – as you can from an office in some high rent, high rated building in the centre of a city?

This 'virtual' law office approach, it was claimed, would mean there was less pressure on law firm accommodation – and smaller offices mean lower overheads. It would allow women lawyers to juggle family life with a professional career. It would help to restore some of the quality of life to lawyers generally. And, with an eye on the bottom line, it would mean that because lawyers spent less time commuting between home and office, they could add a few extra billable hours to their working week. According to one firm, Wilde Sapte, this could amount to 200 extra hours work a year for each lawyer – more than enough to make the system pay for itself.

Unfortunately, in the real world there are concerns about just how compatible telecommuting is with maintaining regular contact with clients. Also, a lot of people simply do not thrive in a working-from-home environment, where the disciplines and rituals of office life are absent. Lawyers really do need to be able to interact with other lawyers, particularly as most large cases and commercial projects are handled by teams rather than individuals.

Although no one would ever admit it, the atmosphere of politics and intrigue within many law firms – particularly among the partners and wannabe partners – is so rife that few lawyers would dare risk their careers by going semi-detached.

Ironically, rather than improving the quality of life for

lawyers, telecommuting technologies have actually made it a lot worse for many. They still have to work in the office but they also have the firm's IT systems in their homes and, thanks to mobile phones and GSM data communications links, they are effectively plugged into the office infrastructure while they commute. In other words they are effectively on call 24 hours a days, seven days a week.

Creating job opportunities for others

Then there are products such as 'fee earner desktop' systems, which have been designed to make all those computers sitting on lawyers' desks gathering dust or serving as display boards for Post-it notes 'more user friendly'.

What this seems to mean in practice is that all those applications – such as access to the accounts records and wordprocessing – that lawyers are already not using, are now available in glorious Technicolour rather than boring old monochrome. And of course these systems are now so complicated that you also need 'help desk' staff to keep them running and IT training staff to ensure everyone knows how to use them properly.

It is the same story with 'litigation support systems'. These were supposedly designed to help lawyers master and keep control of the tens of thousands of documents even the most routine litigation throws up. They now seem to have developed into a job creation scheme for yet more paralegals, as well as students looking to finance their way through law school by spending their evenings, weekends and vacations scanning and coding legal paperwork.

As for the Internet and the world wide web – the latter increasingly termed the 'world wide wait' because it can take so long to locate information – instead of turning into a valuable research facility for lawyers, the growing trend within larger law firms is to insist that all surfing work is delegated to librarians, information officers and other staff familiar with online legal research techniques. (The managing partner of one leading City of London firm has christened these people 'BYTs' – bright, young things. They are just out of university, they know how to operate computers, they are still full of enthusiasm and they work for peanuts.)

Forget concerns about lawyers using the web to tune into sports results or download pornography. They are far too busy for that. The reason why the web is being turned into a no-go-area is exactly the same reason why most firms do not want lawyers to do their own wordprocessing. Their time is too valuable, they are not trained to do it properly and the job can be done in a fraction of the time and for a fraction of the cost by researchers.

This may seem an impressive listing of technologies that have failed to make the killer app grade but we can be certain there will be others. For example, at the time of writing a lot of larger firms are starting to invest substantial amounts of money in the creation of internal 'know-how' systems. Once again, the initial concept is sound – that of capturing the expertise of lawyers and encapsulating it into an easy-to-follow, step-by-step guide to deal with a particular legal problem. It can serve as a training aid for new lawyers and, should your expert have the misfortune to fall under a bus or – worse still – decamp to a competitor, his expertise will not be lost with him.

Most lawyers I have interviewed cringe at the thought of getting involved with these projects because they are far too busy trying to keep on top of their current workloads without the distraction of distilling their expertise for posterity. Nevertheless, the development of know-how systems is providing a lot of useful extra work for IT department staff, legal researchers, BYTs and other information seekers.

But will the legal profession ever find its killer app?

Chapter Four

NO ONE-SIZE-FITS-ALL SOLUTION

There is an old and cruel joke that asks what is the difference between the movie 'Jurassic Park' and the legal technology market. The answer is that one is a high tech adventure playground populated by dinosaurs and the other is a recent film by Steven Spielberg.

So why have the efforts of the last 25 years come to nothing? With the wisdom of hindsight there can now be seen to have been a number of reasons why these various attempts to devise the legal killer app not only never came off, but were probably doomed to fail from the outset.

The usual suspects

It may sound cynical, but in some cases it is now quite clear that the solutions being put forward had more to do with furthering the interests of IT suppliers than improving the quality of life for lawyers. For example, if you can find a reason to put computers on the desktop of every lawyer, then along with the software licence fees, the supplier also stands to make a lot of money from hardware sales, plus training, annual support contracts and the installation of larger networks and servers to support these systems!

There were also problems with 'inappropriate' products that, while meeting the needs of the lawyers who worked in partnership with an IT company to develop the system, (every lawyer likes to think his or her approach is (a) unique and (b) the best of all possible ways of tackling a task) just did not appeal or seem relevant to enough to other lawyers.

Then there are those suppliers who developed systems without apparently ever meeting a real lawyer and thus completely failed to reflect the needs of the profession.

Among the more common mistakes have been IT and software developers failing to appreciate that most solicitors operate as part of a partnership and not a limited company; that the difference between solicitors and barristers is more than a matter of 'one lot wears wigs, while the other lot go into court bare-headed'; that just because a software package is a big hit in Australia or among accountants does not automatically guarantee its appeal to lawyers; that the legal profession is governed by strict professional regulations – such as the 'Solicitors Accounts Rules'; and that even within the UK there are separate legal jurisdictions as both Scotland and Northern Ireland have different systems from the one operating in England and Wales.

As well as suppliers who don't know what lawyers want, there were also those suppliers who chose to work in conjunction with IT and management consultants. The trouble is, most consultants also don't know what lawyers really want but they inevitably have a theory about what lawyers should want. A colleague once commented that consultants are a lot like cushions, they carry the imprint of the last arse – or half-arsed business theory – to have sat on them.

The earlier pre-Windows based systems were also undoubtedly difficult to work with – not so much less than user-friendly as downright user-hostile. By way of further clouding the water, suppliers frequently oversold the benefits of these systems, thus raising expectations to unachievable levels. And they were often expensive and demanded an unrealistic commitment by lawyers in terms of training and system implementation times, to make them work.

Lawyers are busy people and having spent time and money on the selection and purchase of a new computer system (and remember, for lawyers time really is money) they don't take kindly to being told that they then have to spend even more time and money on learning how to use the system and make it work. They want systems that can deliver business solutions – and deliver them now.

Or, to put it another way, many of these contenders for killer app status were doomed from the outset, because they were the wrong systems being supplied to the wrong people at the wrong time.

Blame it on the bean counters

But is there a more fundamental problem, in that the very nature of the legal profession means there can never be a universal one-size-fits-all killer app for lawyers?

The classic model that the whole computer industry seeks to replicate is spreadsheet software. When the 'VisiCalc' and later 'Lotus 1-2-3' programs appeared on the scene in the late 1970s and early 1980s they immediately and almost single-handedly transformed the lives of financial managers and accountants everywhere. They provide software applications whose processes (a) performed a job all bean counters wanted and needed doing, (b) could not be easily duplicated by conventional manual methods, (c) justified the purchase of personal computers and (d) were actually commercially useful.

And if there is a killer system for accountants, surely there should be a similar product for lawyers? But why? It is an old saw that every lawyer thinks they and their own particular areas of legal practice are unique. But there is actually more than an element of truth in it.

Firstly, there is the division between barristers and solicitors – and we should also mention legal executives and licensed conveyancers, as well as the fact that the Scottish and Northern Ireland professions have their own separate legal systems. There is the divide, found on all sides of the profession, between those with primarily paper-based advisory practices and advocates who spend most of their time in courts There is the divide between the different areas of legal work: criminal law, family law, commercial law, between international firms, large 'City' practices and High Street private client practices.

Even the needs of two sole practitioners working from adjacent offices in a small market town may be worlds apart, if one spends all his (or her) time in the local magistrates' court handling Legal Aid work, while the other has, for example, an extensive wills and probate practice.

Is size everything ?

And then there are the dramatic variations in the size, scale and scope of the various 'business units' trading within the legal market, which in turn impact upon both the scale and sophistication of their IT requirements.

Take the example of solicitors' practices. In terms of industry demographics, within the UK there are approximately 10,000 independent law firms. The figure has to be a little vague as each year there is a lot of movement at the very small firm end of the scale with partnerships being formed and dissolved and sole practitioners going in and out of independent practice. (The true figure is also obscured by the fact many firms have semi-autonomous branches practising under different trading names in different towns.)

But, while 10,000 firms may seem a large market, in reality it is very small. There are five very large international practices – known as the 'magic circle' – who between them (according to *Legal Business* magazine) had a total turnover of in excess of £1.25 billion during 1997/98. Next come another five big City of London firms, known as the 'first division', followed by approximately another 15 to 20 firms (the 'second division') plus a growing number of mid-sized 'City', provincial city and 'regional heavyweight' firms.

Add them all together and throughout the whole of the UK there are no more than 100 major law firms which between them employ approximately 30,000 lawyers or about 40 percent of solicitors. (Just five – the magic circle – account for one third of their total turnover).

That leaves another 9,900 other firms accounting for the remaining 60 percent of the profession and once we enter this sector, the size of business unit starts to become much, much smaller. In fact the average size of these firms is just three partners.

Along with the already mentioned 100 major law firms, there are also about 400 reasonable sized commercial practices (together these are known as 'The Legal 500') plus another 1500 substantial 'High Street' firms. But of the remaining 8000, at least 5000 are very small firms – in some instances just sole practitioners – and another 3000 employ less than 10 staff (including all partners, lawyers, other fee earners, secretarial and clerical staff). This contrasts sharply with firms in the 'top 100', where there can be several hundred lawyers alone (the largest employs nearly 1500 fee earners) plus perhaps double that number again by way of secretarial and support staff.

Similarly, many of the City 'mega-practices' have inhouse IT departments employing 30, 40 or 50 staff (which is actually substantially more than the resources available to most legal market software vendors) headed by IT directors on salaries of in excess of £100,000 pa – a sum sole practitioners might take six years to earn from their legal work.

Or, to put it another way, there are only about 2000 'economically active' firms (those having more than 10 staff) in the UK today and they are the only ones who can afford to spend any money on IT or who have a need for front office systems for their lawyers. (Although most of the rest do now have some back office technology, typically accounts systems and wordprocessors, in many instances this can still amount to little more than screen based electronic typewriters. And that is also probably the full extent of their interest in technology, at least for the foreseeable future.)

Given these huge variations, it becomes very difficult to generalise about IT, let alone to try and lay down any hard and fast specifications for a possible universal legal killer app.

The ego has landed
The fact is that while the implementation of certain innovative technologies may prove a catastrophic flop in some firms, in different circumstances and in the hands of other lawyers they can be highly successful. Two examples of this are wordprocessing and speech recognition.

In firms where it makes little or no commercial sense to have lawyers producing their own correspondence, there is no incentive to put a lot of effort into trying to make these technologies succeed. On the other hand those lawyers who cannot afford to employ secretaries, such as sole practitioners or new firms just opening their doors for business, have a very clear incentive (as well as probably more time) to master D-I-Y wordprocessing or to make speech recognition systems work for them.

Probably the best known example of this approach in the UK is the Exeter firm of Rundle Walker. They started from scratch with four partners who all made the effort to learn computer skills themselves, rather than be forced to rely on secretarial or support staff, so they could keep their overheads to a bare minimum and thus afford to compete on price against longer established practices.

Rundle Walker reckon their annual overheads are approximately one-third those of comparable-sized firms of solicitors who still stick with the traditional approach to secretarial and support services. There again, perhaps the partners at Rundle Walker do not have problems with their egos, as it is obvious from the quantity of bored and clearly under-utilised secretarial staff encountered in some larger firms that their primary function is still that of a status symbol or an accoutrement, like the personalised number plates on the BMW, that go with being a partner.

Even the geographical location of a firm can make a significant difference between the success or failure of a particular technology. For example, a firm in the London area, where secretarial salaries are notoriously high, has an incentive to maximise the use of fee earner support technologies, so lawyers are less reliant on secretaries.

Indeed, reducing the length of the 'administrative tail' – in other words the ratio of fee earners to non-fee earners in a firm – is a key strategy for any conscientious practice manager. Apart from having the potential to cut the wages bill, it can also have an impact on office accommodation (less people to accommodate means less building space is required) and on expansion strategies. You can hire additional lawyers without worrying whether they will generate enough in extra fees to pay for the corresponding number of additional support staff you will also have to hire.

Evidence suggests that whereas in smaller (and almost inevitably less efficient) law firms there may be a 1:2 ratio of fee earners to non-fee earners (in better managed firms a 1:1 ratio is the norm), the use of technology can change this to 2:1, 3:1, 4:1 or even, according to one legal aid practice I visited in the East End of London, a ratio of 5:1.

Alternatively, in rural areas and other parts of the UK, where not only are secretarial salaries relatively low but it is also difficult to recruit suitably qualified professional staff, a firm may well adopt the opposite strategy of installing IT systems so that secretaries and clerical staff take on an increasing fee earning role.

Once again there have been some notable success stories, such as the sole practitioner in Kent who, thanks to a case management system and a team of a dozen non legally qualified computer operators working eight hour shifts, now has a turnover of over half-a-million pounds a year generated from handling mortgage arrears work for building societies.

By way of an interesting permutation on this fee earners-as-secretaries versus secretaries-as-fee earners debate, a number of central London firms are now trying to get the best of both worlds.

Their London offices operate primarily as the venue for meetings between lawyers and clients, with support staff kept to a minimum. At one practice there is just a single receptionist/PA. Meanwhile out in their country offices, where both salary levels and office rents are lower, there is the usual complement of secretaries and clerical staff.

Thanks to high speed telecommunications links and similar telecommuter technologies, the service the lawyers receive from their 'remote' office 100 miles away is exactly the same as if their support staff were sitting next door in the same London office block. (Another solicitors' practice – niche City law firm Davis & Co – recently won a 'bronze' award in the 1998 *Lawyer*/HIFAL awards for its use of extranet and telecommuting technologies to create a virtual office environment.)

Commoditise, productise and systemise

This same phenomenon – that one law firm's IT success story is another practice's computing disaster – can also be seen in the experiences of users of case management technology.

Cut through the hype surrounding these systems and it becomes evident that the more successful implementations are in those firms that have been willing to repackage and re-engineer the way they deliver legal services.

Management consultants will tell you that this involves the 'commoditisation' or 'productisation and systemisation' of the law – a move away from providing legal services on a one-to-one basis, with the handling of each matter or project individually tailored to meet the specific needs of that client, and the development instead of generic legal 'products' that can be supplied on a one-to-many basis.

This is true. But it is also essentially the same 'pile 'em high and sell them cheap' philosophy that has been successfully employed over the years by everyone from market traders through to car manufacturers.

If you can develop a viable automated workflow for processing a particular class of legal work – such as uninsured loss recovery, motor insurance claims ('bent bumper' cases), Consumer Credit Act debt collection – you are in a position to (a) handle large volumes of work and thus win business that might not otherwise come your way, (b) reduce the unit cost of handling this work, so you can afford to compete on price but still make an acceptable profit margin, and (c) still maintain the management and quality controls that are essential in law firms.

The Scottish law firm Morton Fraser recently claimed that its use of case management technology within a specially created department to handle high volumes of 'commodity' legal work had 'more than halved' operating costs. Another practice – Dibb Lupton Alsop – reckons that along with saving costs, (including a reduction in its administrative tail ratio from 1:1 to 4:1) the introduction of a new commoditised case management system in its defendant personal injury practice resulted in a 10 to 20 percent increase in fee income.

Clearly there are success stories, but this does not make case management the profession's legal 'killer application'.

It only works in certain types of practice, namely those that are prepared to commit the resources in terms of business process re-engineering. It only works when handling certain classes of legal work. It is only relevant for firms that are interested in winning high volume, relatively low margin business. And, of course, it is yet another technology that primarily benefits paralegals and legal practices as business entities, but does nothing for individual lawyers.

The fact is that the legal business is so diverse in terms of the size of practices, the type of work being handled and the differing needs of practitioners that there is not and can never be a universal one-size-fits-all killer app that will benefit all lawyers. At best, one lawyer's IT success story is another practitioner's 'so-what-who-cares?' technology.

But, could this be about to change and should lawyers be following a different approach? Before going on to answer these questions, we first need to consider the impact of the so-called digital communications revolution and its role as an enabling technology.

Chapter Five

TWINKLE TWINKLE LITTLE MODEM STATUS LIGHT

Lenin, among others, is reported to have said that revolutions are a lot like omelettes in that you cannot have one without breaking a few eggs. The question worrying a lot of lawyers today is whether recent trends in technology will consign them to the chafing dish of history.

Whether you are reading about it in newspaper supplements or watching television programmes on the subject, whenever the topic of computer technology crops up today, almost inevitably you will also encounter the increasingly hackneyed phrase, the 'digital communications revolution'.

Digital communications revolution – what revolution? And what has any of this to do with either the legal profession or the practice of law?

Good questions. Not least because too often the sum total of these amazing advances in technology appears to amount to little more than giving school kids in Slough the ability to download hard core pornography off the Internet, while their parents sit at home using online services to order fresh fromage frais from the local supermarket. Underwhelming or what?

So what is digital communications technology? How does it differ from other forms of information technology? And why should its advent be heralded as a revolution?

The first byte

Without delving too deeply into electronic engineering principles, in the world of information technology – which, among other things, encompasses computing, telephony, CD-Rom, data communications, image processing, video conferencing and multimedia systems – there are two contrasting approaches to transferring signals from one device to another.

The traditional approach (traditional only in that it dates back to the later years of the nineteenth century) is analogue (or analog) communications in which a voice message, sound recording or data is transmitted as a continuously varying wave. Currently almost all radio and television services in the UK are analogue – although this is soon to change. The older fixed (British Telecom) and mobile (cellular) telephone networks that are now being phased out are also analogue, as are vinyl records and audio cassette tapes.

The alternative and newer approach is digital communications in which a signal is broken down into a series of discrete binary codes. Actually it is a series of zeros (0s) and ones (1s) because technology of this kind only understands two things: power on (1) and power off (0).

For example, with 8-bit binary code (eight bits equals one byte) the letter 'A' is coded as '01000001'. This may seem a limitation but in fact 8-bit code provides a total of 256 different combinations of 0s and 1s, while a more advanced 24-bit code can provide 16.7 million permutations. (If you look at the on/off switches on most items of office technology – faxes, photocopiers, printers and computers – you will see the 'on' position is marked with a '1' symbol and the 'off' with a '0'.) Relax, that's it, no more deep techie stuff.

Now it may seem strange to have a communications medium based on a technology that appears about as sophisticated as standing by an electric light and flicking the switch on and off to create a form of visual morse code. But in fact, because digital signals are transmitted as a series of regular bite-sized chunks, it is far easier for the device at the receiving end of the process to reconstruct the signal exactly as it was sent.

This sounds like gibberish, but as with all forms of business technology, it is not the technical nitty-gritty – the rams, roms and under-the-bonnet stuff – that matters but the practical implications of such developments. In other words, what can you do with it and how does it improve on what has gone before ?

Digital technology is 'cleaner' than its analogue counterpart. (You only have to compare the sound quality of a digital compact disc with the same piece of music recorded on an analogue vinyl LP, which is admittedly fine for grand opera or Oasis but of little relevance to office automation.) But the big advantage of digital communications over analogue signals is that you can do so much more with it. In other words you really can get several bites (or bytes) out of the same cherry.

Thus older analogue technology is inherently inflexible when you want to transfer information between different platforms. Take the example of fax machines and the way they operated across the old analogue telephone network.

You might create and print out a perfect-looking document on your wordprocessor, which you then fed into a fax, where the image of the document was 'digitised' into an electronic signal format prior to transmission to the intended recipient's fax machine. But, because the telecoms link between the two systems was an analogue line, your fax machine's modem would first have to translate the digital signal into an analogue format. And, in turn, the recipient's modem would then have to translate the analogue signal back into a digital format prior to printing out your message.

Given the circumstances of all this electronic translation rigmarole, far from being surprised and annoyed that sometimes the fax messages we received were distorted by interference, a more appropriate response would be amazement that fax machines ever worked at all!

This unsatisfactory state of affairs is in complete contrast with digital technology, where an enormous number of seemingly unrelated devices have the potential for seamless mutual data communication. Computers, cell phones, pagers, printers, scanners, LCD projectors, faxes, video conferencing, personal organisers, VCRs, television and even digital cameras are all part of the same family and talk the same language.

To use a hypothetical example: suppose you have a personal injuries client who has tripped over a broken paving slab and now wants to make a substantial compensation claim against the appropriate local government authority.

As part of your case preparation work, you might have a conventional photograph taken of the offending object for use in evidence and – once the film was properly developed – send a copy by post to the authority along with a letter before action. You might also have additional copies made for sending to counsel and all the other parties involved in the action.

But that is about as far as you can go without bringing in additional technology to process the photograph in different ways. Once a photograph, always a photograph.

On the other hand, you could have the photograph taken with a digital camera and in addition to printing off a hard copy version, within minutes of taking the picture, you could be incorporating the image directly within the body of a wordprocessed letter to be posted or faxed to other parties. Alternatively, you might want to download it into a computer for sending to the other side as an 'attachment' to an email message warning them of your intention to sue.

Why stop there? If the claim is being disputed and looks like heading for litigation, you could add the photographic image to a CD-Rom disk as part of the 'virtual' trial bundle of digitised documents you send to counsel. And, assuming a satisfactory conclusion to the case, if your practice intends to specialise in this kind of work, you could even incorporate the image within your firm's promotional material on an Internet web site or on a PowerPoint style slide, as part of a marketing presentation at a professional seminar.

True, you could do the same thing with a conventional photograph but it would take time – several days at least – and you would also have to run to the expense of sending the job to an outside specialist processing bureau. Now contrast this with digital technology where the tools are cheap – most will already be there on your desktop PC and the whole process is very quick, in some cases only a few mouse 'clicks' away.

From offshore islands to the global village

Over the last few years we have grown accustomed to hearing about the potential benefits of personal computers. But there is a limitation, in that these are essentially individual productivity tools to be used in a stand alone capacity. Although they may help us process raw data into more digestible gobbets of information, the true value of this information lies not in its mere possession but in its use – and data is of little use to anyone if it remains locked up within the narrow confines of your desktop hardware.

With digital technology, however, we are not only seeing systems that are more flexible and easier to use, but which also have an inherent communications ability.

Instead of just personal productivity, we now have technology that allows us to share information and collaborate on common projects with other people. Thanks to advanced communications technologies, including the Internet and electronic mail, these people can be your colleagues within the same law firm, instructed counsel in their chambers, expert witnesses, insurance companies, building societies, local authorities, courts and all those other contacts who can be drawn into the most routine of non-contentious matters – or even a client located on the far side of the globe.

Instead of remote offshore islands of information, digital communications technology is opening the way towards the creation of a low cost, truly easy to use online global village – an online global village in which lawyers have the potential to be vital members of the community.

Digital technology makes life a whole lot simpler and more convenient for everyone toiling at the electronic interface by facilitating the convergence of previously incompatible technologies – and the Internet is the lubricating oil that makes everything run smoothly.

Welcome to the revolution

This still leaves unanswered the question of why all these developments should be heralded as a revolution. Perhaps it is the word 'revolution' that is misleading.

There is a tendency to see all revolutions as being relatively short-term political events. A few shots from the Red Guard are all that is needed to storm the Winter Palace – and that's the Russian Revolution over, bar the shouting and the show trials. Perhaps a more appropriate model is that of the Industrial Revolution which began in the UK in the first half of the eighteenth century and was still rumbling along over a century later.

By comparison, the computing revolution is still in its infancy. For example, what is generally regarded as the world's first commercial production line computer – the IBM 603 Calculator –

was launched in March 1946. On the communications front, direct dialling to the USA only started in 1967 and the beginnings of what we now call the Internet go back to 1969 – forget Oasis, the Beatles were still playing then.

The first microprocessor made its debut in 1971. And the original DOS plus Intel 8088/86 processor-based IBM PC (the direct forerunner of today's office PCs) did not appear for another decade, in 1981. As for the world wide web, that was unheard of in 1990, while other technologies that are now seen as being business critical – notably intranets and extranets – were words that had not even been coined a couple of years ago.

Turning to the future, although we have seen the computing revolution penetrate big and medium-sized businesses, commerce, industry, government and, more recently, the educational, SOHO (small office/home office) and professional sectors, it has still barely touched the domestic consumer market. But it will.

Perhaps not immediately. But, as new technologies that are only just starting to emerge – such as interactive digital television, due to be launched in the UK in the latter part of 1998 – begin to gain a critical mass during the first years of the next century, so the digital world will become a truly mass market media.

You may be lucky. You may have been running your legal practice along outdated business lines for the last decade and still be holding your commercial head above water. But the digital communications revolution is surely coming and treading water won't be enough once everyone else is equipped with flippers and goggles and powering along several lengths ahead of you in the fast lane.

Once people start turning to online systems to search for providers of professional services such as lawyers, in the same way that they currently look through telephone directories and newspaper ads, it will radically transform – in fact revolutionise – the way we all operate.

Chapter Six

JOIN THE MARTINI GENERATION

"Consumers' expectations are changing with their lifestyles. Cash rich, time poor customers in particular need access to services and goods outside normal office hours. The companies who are responding to this are already taking market share by offering more choice and convenience."
BARRY BONNETT, BRITISH TELECOMMUNICATIONS

So, one of the consequences of the digital communications revolution is that the Internet is going to play a more important role in all our lives? Consider the facts...

According to the results of a survey conducted by management consultants KPMG in association with US publisher Ziff-Davis, by May 1998 the number of adults in the UK – and hence potential clients of lawyers – using the Internet had reached six million people or 13 percent of the total population. Six million is an impressive figure in its own right but what makes this really interesting is that it is double – a whole 100 percent increase – the number of people who were using it in May 1997.

The Consumers' Association offshoot *Which? Online* puts the May 1998 figure at already over seven million and other studies suggest more people are going online at a rate of 10,000 households per week. NOP Research estimate the number of UK users will reach nine million by early 1999.

These figures are likely to be further boosted by the supermarket chain Tesco, which has announced its intention to become a low-cost Internet service provider (ISP) – the sub-text here being that it will help encourage use of Tesco's online shopping services; and by British Telecommunications, which is now planning a subscription-free, pay-as-you-go Internet access service called BT Click as an alternative to the more conventional approach of taking out a monthly contract with an ISP. BT is aiming this service at the estimated two million households in the UK that have Internet-capable PCs but have not yet signed up with an ISP. The cost is expected to be as little as 1p per minute on top of the normal BT local call rate and users will also be able to sign up for BT's free email service.

As to the prospects for future growth, the potential is enormous. For example, at the moment the majority of people accessing the Internet are either enthusiasts connecting from home or business/professionals (including the academic community) connecting from the workplace.

The feature common to both groups is that they are all, almost without exception, connecting via personal computers. But, personal computers are not a mass market domestic product – in 1997 more than four million televisions were bought in the UK compared with just 1.6 million consumer PCs.

If you want to reach the mass market it therefore follows that you must approach them by the TV not the PC – and this is about to happen. There are a growing number of non-PC Internet access technologies, including network computers (NCs) and coin-operated web browsing terminals in public places, such as libraries and even pubs. The first of these are already in use, and there is also the promise of an 'Internet phone' device from BT. However, probably the most exciting innovation is interactive digital television, which will have some form of Internet access facility included with the set-top boxes (STBs) that serve as the digital signal decoders.

(Recognising that a lot of people still cannot get a video recorder to work properly, Microsoft and Lernout & Hauspie, a Belgian speech recognition company, are even working on a voice-activated interface for STBs that will actually allow you to surf the Internet using spoken commands. In a related development, Microsoft's WebTV Networks division and the BBC have announced they are to commence extensive trials of an interactive television service in the UK that will give TV viewers access to a 'web page locator feature' providing quick and easy access to web sites that are directly related to TV programmes.)

The first of the new generation of digital television networks will go live in the UK from the autumn of 1998, but it will probably be the spring of 1999 before these services – such as British Interactive Broadcasting (BIB), which is backed by both BT and Midland Bank among others – start moving into the mainstream. Nevertheless, it is already being predicted that by the year 2001, just two years away, over 15 percent of domestic Internet access will be via non-PC technologies.

In their report *Network Computing: Opportunities for the Consumer Market,* UK technology analysts Ovum comment: "Most people today use a personal computer as the access device for receiving on-line information. However, PCs are relatively expensive and complex.

"The complication of setting up and managing the system and ensuring the software is up to date is a daunting challenge to the consumer. The user interface needs to be more familiar to people. We therefore believe that the TV will be the first choice as a vehicle for non-PC data service access.

"People are already familiar with the TV as a means of receiving information and entertainment. Augmenting this experience with data from the Internet is the next logical step."

From couch potatoes to surf watchers

While it can be argued that because the Internet has blossomed so rapidly, it is difficult to predict where it will be or what form it will take in even a couple of years' time (and it is worth remembering that even Microsoft supremo Bill Gates initially underestimated the role and growth of the Internet) one thing is clear: the Internet is moving from the fringes to the mainstream of all our lives, in the same way that, for example, in the space of less than a decade the mobile phone has moved from being an expensive accessory for well-heeled yuppies, to a device every school kid now seems to carry in a shoulder bag.

From being the hobby for the 'early adopters' of novel (and in some instances just plain 'novelty') technologies, it is now emerging as a mass market consumer service on a par with television and the telephone.

Or, to put it another way: if the people using the Internet today equate to the managers of those businesses that make up the commercial client lists of 'The Legal 500', the households that are now starting to come online equate to the private clients of High Street firms. It is for precisely these reasons that the legal profession must wake up, smell the coffee and be prepared for the changes that are coming.

As with all new technologies, usage patterns tend to begin with non-essential experiments. With mobile phones the first thing we all did was phone our friends and family to say, "Hey, I've got a mobile phone and I'm calling you from a train making its way from York to Edinburgh". But, once the initial novelty wore off, we switched to using them primarily for business purposes.

It is the same with the Internet. The initial reaction to the world wide web is to surf about with no particular destination in mind and follow up every hyperlink that crosses our path. When the novelty wears off, it starts to be used for more 'serious' purposes, such as academic or business research to locate items of information that cannot be found by more conventional methods. Increasingly too, it is used as a commercial medium for buying or requesting further information about products and services.

This latter aspect – known as electronic commerce (or e-commerce) – is widely predicted to become the Internet's primary function within the next few years. For example, in 1997 the total value of business transactions conducted globally across the Internet amounted to US$ 3 billion. According to the US research consultancy IDC, by 2002 this figure will have increased to US$ 333 billion with perhaps 60 million people online in Europe alone. (IDC also estimates that the value of e-commerce revenue generated in the UK will be worth £2.7 billion by the year 2005.)

So how are people using the Internet today?

They are using it as a giant reference source, in effect a global *Yellow Pages*, for locating the suppliers of products and services – even to-your-door pizza delivery services.

They are using it as a way of ordering and in some instances paying (via secure credit card transactions) for those products and services. Currently the most frequently purchased items are computers, software and books. The computer manufacturer Dell, which now gets over 100,000 visits a week to its European web site, says sales of PC hardware via the Internet are now generating US$ 1 million a day in revenue from Europe alone.

They are using it to track and monitor the progress and fulfilment of the products and services they have ordered. One of the best known examples of this is the Federal Express (FedEx) parcels service in the USA, which has an interactive web facility allowing customers to track the progress of their parcels from initial pick-up, through various shipping stations across North America and finally on to when it was delivered and who signed for it.

And they are using it to monitor the financial

consequences of buying these various products and services. For example, a growing number of banks in the UK now offer Internet-based online banking services that allow customers to check account balances and transactions, pay bills and transfer funds between accounts.

(A new study *Banking in Europe* by Dr Elizabeth Daniel of City University predicts that, thanks to rising home PC ownership and Internet connections, the demand for electronic banking services in the UK will rise by more than 30 percent a year until 2005. More than one-in-seven customers are expected to be using the Internet, PC banking or interactive television to carry out their banking transactions.)

But why should this be of any interest to lawyers?

As the digital communications revolution rolls on its way, one-time niche technologies, such as the Internet, are rapidly moving into the mainstream. This in turn is having a significant impact upon the user market. From relatively small numbers of IT enthusiasts, early adopters and aficionados (the so-called 'digiterati') we are now seeing the emergence of a far broader digitally street-wise audience: the 'Martini generation'.

They have the technology, they understand how to use it and they know it has the ability to deliver the right answers to the right people at 'any time, any place, anywhere'.

They are now coming to expect the prospective suppliers of the goods and services they are interested in to be equally wired up and web enabled as they are. And if suppliers are not sufficiently digitally aware to be able to provide the interactive service levels consumers are demanding, they are likely to switch their allegiance to suppliers who can.

If you can search the web for new insurance cover or estate agents' property particulars, why can't you also search it for details of solicitors' practices and other providers of legal services?

If you can order and pay for books and computers via

the web, why can't you also send new instructions to a solicitor, obtain a quotation on how much it will cost to have a firm handle a conveyancing transaction for you, or make and pay for a new will?

If you can monitor the progress of a parcel as it makes its way from Seattle to Savannah, why can't you use the web to find out if the company you are suing for bad debts has paid up, made an offer or otherwise responded to the 'letter before action' from your lawyers?

If you can communicate with a supplier via email or an interactive web site from anywhere in the world and at any time of the day or night, why can't you contact your lawyer after 5.00pm on a Friday evening until sometime during the following Monday morning?

And, if you can log on to your bank's web site to see if your salary cheque has been paid into your account, why can't you also log on to your lawyer's client account records to see how much of your money has already been spent pursuing some ongoing litigation?

What we are seeing is a revolution in communications. Just as face-to-face meetings and correspondence by post has been superseded on a day-to-day basis by fax and telephone communications, so we are now moving into an era when Internet email, web sites and other forms of digital communication (such as video conferencing) are becoming the expected norm.

At the time of writing there are only about 400 law firms within the whole UK that have their own web sites. But, given the current momentum of digital technologies, within three years interactive web sites and Internet email addresses will have become as essential to law firms as fax machines and the telephone are today. Or, should I say essential to all those firms who don't want to slip into the twilight zone currently occupied by sunset practices.

Chapter Seven

IT'S THE CLIENTS, STUPID!

According to the sixties Black Power activist Adam Clayton Powell: "A man's respect for law and order exists in precise relationship to the size of his paycheck". Perhaps that is true but it is also that paycheck that keeps lawyers in business.

Time now to start drawing the various strands in this book together: the quest for the legal killer app; the third-way of legistics and post millennium realism; the impact of the digital communications revolution; and the growth of a new market of Martini generation consumers. What are the practical consequences for lawyers – or is this just more technology to spend money on and receive little or no benefit in return?

Although the last 25 years have seen a growing emphasis being placed upon the distinction between 'front office' and 'back office' law office automation systems, not only have they made very little practical difference to the way lawyers actually work (eg the singular failure to find a universal legal killer app) but as far as the real world is concerned they are essentially internal, inward looking support technologies. And, as such, for all practical purposes they are totally irrelevant to lawyers' clients and prospective clients.

By way of explanation, consider the experiences of the UK retail banking sector. One of the big success stories in recent times has been the launch and growth of First Direct, the telephone banking division of the Midland Bank/HSBC Group. Now, to have been able to start from scratch and build up a successful banking operation within the space of a few years suggests First Direct must have some very good internal IT systems.

They must have a good marketing system to be able to identify and maintain contact with prospective customers, as well as the equivalent of a client database to look after the current account holders' records.

They must have good internal accounts systems for processing all the payments going in and out of customer accounts and for ensuring that any deductions for bank charges and interest payments are accurately identified, calculated and allocated.

They must have the equivalent of diary reminder/workflow management software to ensure direct debit and standing order instructions are paid in or out of customer accounts on the correct date and for the correct amount.

They must also have a smooth document production system – the banking equivalent of wordprocessing – to produce and send out neatly printed statements each month.

And, they must have a good document management system so they can locate and dispatch extra copies of statements when they are requested by customers.

But, frankly, who cares? I did not open an account with First Direct because they had all this backroom support technology lurking under the bonnet. The reason I switched to First Direct was because of the value added services they could offer – which in this case was a 24-hours-a-day, 365-days a year telephone banking facility.

Of course the accurate processing of transactions going through my account is important, as is their ability to handle my direct debits without a hitch and send me accurate statements each month, but I assume that as a modern bank First Direct, in common with all the other retail banks, would provide these 'support' services as a matter of course.

Now compare and contrast the situation that prevails at over 99 percent of law firms in the UK. Almost all their IT projects and expenditure are directed towards inward looking systems. But, once again, who really cares?

A commercial client does not take new business to a City firm because they like the look of the correspondence it produces using Microsoft Word 97, or because they are impressed to learn that partners have desktop access to online legal information services. No, they go there because they know (or at least hope) they will receive the best possible advice.

In fact as long as the service is good, most clients – commercial or private – probably couldn't care less if a law firm's entire document production was in the hands of a bunch of chimpanzees sitting at manual typewriters and taking time off from recreating the works of Shakespeare.

The human resources directors (as personnel department managers now prefer to be called) within large law firms talk about the importance of a practice's support facility (IT, secretarial, library, accounts, paralegals) being able to deliver a good service to their 'customers'. By that they mean the partners, solicitors and other fee earners who rely on these support services but the only 'customers' who really matter are the clients!

In the circumstances, it is hardly surprising that the legal profession has not yet managed to find a killer app and has had a frequently less than satisfactory experience with IT. It has spent the last 25 years approaching the subject from the wrong direction. Lawyers have been throwing all their energies (and money) into inward looking technologies when they should have been following the example of some of their competitors (including banks, insurance companies and estate agents) and concentrating on outward looking, client-facing systems.

The legal world has devoted a quarter of a century to looking for systems to make life easier for lawyers (supply led applications) whereas they should have been concentrating on systems to meet the needs of their clients (demand led applications).

Chapter Eight

COME THE HOUR, COME THE TECHNOLOGY

"The first principle of management is that the driving force for the development of new products is not technology, nor money but the imagination of people."
DAVID PACKARD

"OK," you say, "perhaps we did get it wrong in the past but why should now be any different?"

The important – and for some firms no doubt worrying – feature about the current legal services market is the convergence of two key trends – the sea change in client attitudes towards lawyers and the impact of digital technology.

Clients are no longer prepared to treat their legal advisers with deference and accept services in whatever format they are delivered. Instead, more and more are starting to make demands as to how and when their needs are met.

In addition, a growing proportion of both commercial and private clients now know that technologies such as the Internet and extranets exist and can provide a simple communications link between otherwise incompatible technologies. This is in contrast with the days of the old proprietary IT systems, when commercial clients knew from their own computing experiences that trying to forge links with outside organisations, such as law firms, usually involved more trouble and expense than it was worth.

Draw the two trends together and a situation arises in which clients now have the potential to dictate the way in which law firms conduct business with them.

Currently most of the running is being made by larger commercial clients, who usually have their own inhouse legal departments and a sophisticated approach to buying external legal services. But the same demands are starting to be made by smaller businesses and, with the rise of the Martini generation, eventually we can expect to see even private clients making these demands of High Street practices.

A competitive market is a buyer's market and in a buyer's market the consumer is king. The traditional lawyer/client balance has changed, probably forever. We are now living in the age of client 'pull' and any law firms which are not prepared, or which lack the imagination to meet those demands, risk seeing their clients defect to more accommodating competitors – be they other law firms or alternative suppliers of legal services.

SWOT analysis

The natural reaction of many law firms to the idea that they may in some way have to open up their IT systems to the outside world – or at least to their clients – is that this is a complete anathema. But if you actually consider the options calmly and subject it to a SWOT (strengths, weaknesses, opportunities and threats) analysis, the potential benefits by far outweigh any perceived disadvantages.

For example, two of the most common questions clients ask of their legal advisers are: "Where have we got to with a particular matter?" (in other words progress reporting and matter tracking) and "How much of our money have you spent?" (client balance and financial reporting).

Currently both questions have to be answered by either lawyers or their staff. It is inconvenient for them, as it is an interruption that may distract them from getting on with other higher billing value added tasks. It is also inconvenient for the client as they cannot have access to the information when they want it – and they probably want it now – but instead have to wait until their legal advisers get back to them with the information. This can be particularly difficult if the client is dealing with one of the more traditional High Street firms (about 90 percent of the UK legal profession) which still works 9-til-5 hours and closes for the whole weekend.

With digital communications the answers to both these questions can be handled electronically. In the case of a larger commercial client, typically one for whom lawyers may be handling a number of similar matters (such as 'commoditised' high volume, low margin debt collection work) on their behalf, it is now possible to give the client access to selected information contained in the firm's accounts or case management database systems, by means of an extranet. (This is a secure, private information sharing network that uses the same web browser software and hypertext-based page structure as the public Internet.)

On the other hand, for smaller firms handling private client work, a more convenient and cost effective approach may be to 'publish' regularly updated financial and status reports onto a secure, password protected site on the public Internet. The actual nuts and bolts of the system are irrelevant. What is important is that the necessary technology is already available – all that is needed is the willingness to use it.

In terms of benefits, as well as being more convenient – no more interruption for the lawyer and the client can access the information to fit in with their time scales and agenda (a particularly important factor if you are dealing with international clients) – this approach also addresses one of the most frequently raised grievances about the legal profession which is poor communications.

The latest of many reports on this subject is a research study conducted by Bristol University which found that 55 percent of all complaints made about solicitors in England and Wales related to lack of proper communications. With a properly configured Internet or extranet service, the communications onus shifts to the client – the information is there and can be collected at their convenience. (The Legal Services Ombudsman has also warned that it is high time lawyers "put their own houses in order, particularly with regard to how they communicated with clients".)

Technologies of this kind may even help achieve what is known among marketing people as a 'virtuous circle'. An example of this could be an online progress reporting facility: the service benefits the law firm because it means clients are no longer interrupting lawyers for routine reports. The service benefits the clients because they can get the information they need without having to ask the lawyers to provide it. Thus both sides benefit from the investment in the technology – and both sides have a positive incentive to continue using it.

The demand is out there

Do clients really want such a service? According to a recent survey conducted on behalf of the Institute of Directors they certainly do – the results found that speed of response was perceived as the key benefit of using the Internet by 56 percent of the businesses in the sample. And yet there are even large City law firms that still forbid their fee earners to make contact with the outside world via email!

A further insight into the needs of clients is to be found in the results of a survey conducted by research consultancy CSS in the early summer of 1998. According to *Image and Performance of Legal Advisers 1998,* over 80 percent of the heads of inhouse legal departments and other major buyers of legal services in the UK expect technology will "significantly change the way legal services are provided".

Over half of those expecting change are interested in faster and more efficient communications, particularly greater use of email. Perhaps more significantly, the survey also found that a high proportion of respondents 'spontaneously' volunteered the opinion that they would like the law firms they used to deliver better technological solutions. One criticism made was that many law firm web sites contain just advertorial 'window dressing' rather than informative legal material.

Along with better communications, two other technologies attracting the interest of legal services buyers were the ability to download precedents and other legal documents directly from the Internet and the ability to access law firm online information and library services. As one participant in the survey put it: "Being an inhouse lawyer, the thing you lack is access to a library, so if that is something outside law firms can sell you, that makes quite a lot of sense. It won't reduce the amount of work you give them and in fact it means you spot more issues."

City law firm Linklaters is already running an online legal information service called 'Blue Flag' (see page 86) that meets part of this demand and Dibb Lupton Alsop recently launched a research service for inhouse legal departments wanting to take advantage of the firm's extensive online, CD and conventional library resources, as well as its team of full-time research staff.

The report ends with the ominous conclusion by CSS that in the past two years since the last survey was conducted "there has been a significant attitudinal shift and technology is now a major issue". With "significant numbers" of inhouse lawyers already using the Internet and a massive 73 percent planning to make greater use of it during the next twelve months "this suggests fast change and law firms will have to react quickly to keep up with expectations".

Finally, a survey carried out by chartered accountants James & Cowper, in association with the LawNet group of independent solicitors' practices, found that there was "clear client pressure" for lawyers to get online and start communicating electronically via email and related technologies.

The survey's authors predict that the next three years will see increasing client demand for law firms to provide "gateways to limited access into inhouse information systems" and suggests practices that embrace these systems will gain a competitive advantage in the delivery of client services. The survey also anticipates that web-enabled systems, including intranets and extranets, will play a growing role in the delivery of legal services.

Interestingly, a lot of this pressure is coming from inhouse lawyers, who are now widely seen as the main buyers of corporate legal services.

Not that long ago inhouse legal practice was seen as the soft underbelly of the legal world. It was condescendingly seen as a place where lawyers who were not going to make partnership grade in private practice but still wanted to be called 'solicitor' on their business cards, went for an easy life.

Times have changed. Inhouse lawyers are now usually better organised, more efficiently run, better funded and have a superior IT infrastructure to their counterparts in private practice.

A window on the world

But why stop there? As well as providing an interactive reporting facility, there are plenty of other opportunities now opening up thanks to digital technology.

Prospective clients can seek quotations for new work – a number of firms are now providing interactive quotes for conveyancing work via their web sites. New instructions can be lodged either via an extranet in the case of an existing corporate client, or via the public Internet in the case of a new private client. The north London firm of Kaye Tesler has now been offering will drafting and other similar relatively straightforward legal services to the general web surfing public since 1996. (Solicitor Michael Kaye is a long-time pioneer of innovative legal technologies and also runs a number of successful IT ventures – his firm was another of the winners in the 1998 *Lawyer*/HIFAL awards.)

And then there is the chance to plug into the bigger picture. In a competitive market where, from the prospective client's point of view, there is very little to distinguish one law firm from another, having even the most rudimentary web site can give a firm an edge and help differentiate it from the competition.

As a marketing tool there is an obvious advantage in terms of the positive, modern image conveyed by being digitally aware, compared with firms that are still stuck in the postage stamps and fountain pens era. However, while this might be dismissed as just hype, the world wide web is just that – a global entity in which a law firm's web site can act as a shop window for its services that is open 24 hours a day and can be accessed at anytime by anyone from anywhere on the planet.

For firms offering services to an international client base – and this encompasses not just big City firms targeting multinationals, but also smaller practices wanting to sell private client services to expatriates – this provides opportunities to reach prospects who could never be located by conventional advertising or direct mail campaigns. Closer to home, lawyers with highly specialised practices and firms handling referrals business have reported a similar knock-on effect, in that they are now attracting work from far outside their traditional, relatively narrow catchment area.

Barristers are lawyers too

So far barristers have not featured too heavily in this book because (a) in terms of their numbers, as well as their use of and expenditure on IT they are a relatively small proportion of the legal profession and (b) they only have an indirect relationship with the ultimate end user of legal services: the client. (Except for those professions that have direct access to the Bar, the barrister is instructed by a solicitor who is, in turn, instructed by the lay client.)

It therefore also follows that as most solicitors have not yet woken up to the shift in the client/lawyer balance, the Bar is probably even more out of touch with the commercial pressures circulating in the real world. Nevertheless, during the course of researching this book I found enough evidence to support the view that consumerism is also heading towards the Inns of Court and that the view among lay clients is that he who pays the piper should be able to call at least some of the tunes.

The major cause of grievance is the conference system, which inevitably requires both the client and the instructing solicitor to visit the barrister in his or her set of chambers. If the barrister in question is a senior silk (QC) or practices in one of the more rarefied fields of law, this usually means a trip to chambers in London.

Despite the fact that they are paid to attend conferences, (albeit for Legal Aid practitioners at a lower rate than they could earn for other types of legal work,) solicitors have long complained that the conference system wastes time on travel and is an unwelcome diversion from working on more profitable matters – the value added argument again. However, it is now being recognised that clients too value their time and would much rather be getting on with their lives or running their businesses than attending meetings with their legal advisors.

The technology now being championed by the Bar Council, among others, is video conferencing. The argument here is that barristers, solicitors, clients, witnesses, judges and potentially every part of the justice system could save a considerable amount of time and money if, instead of having this legal circus travelling around the country to attend routine meetings, conferences and court proceedings, the majority of these face-to-face transactions could be conducted just as easily via a video conference link.

The sticking point seems to be that while the spirit is willing, the bank balance is weak and further progress has currently ground to a halt over the issue of who is going to pay for the technology.

Perhaps barristers (as distinct from the Bar Council who, to give them their due, really have put a lot of effort into trying to promote the use of this technology) will realise that if they hope to win or retain business against competition both from other chambers (there is a lot of rivalry between London and provincial sets) and the growing number of solicitor advocates, they are going to have to buy these systems for themselves.

In fact a number of sets have already taken the plunge and invested in video conferencing and similar types of client facing technology (voice mail also has its adherents). These are now enjoying considerable success in winning and retaining new firms of instructing solicitors. But too many other barristers have yet to realise that the rosy glow they see in the west is not the light at the end of the tunnel but the sun about to set on their professional careers.

The ties that bind

At the most basic level, the offspring of the digital communications revolution – technologies such as the Internet and video conferencing (it is also possible to carry out fairly basic video conferencing across the web) – have the potential to provide a useful interactive communications link between lawyers and their clients. However, there are also other benefits.

Interactive technologies can help build and reinforce partnerships with complementary service providers. In the mergers and acquisitions field, these might include merchant banks, stockbrokers and other financial institutions. In the litigation arena, potential partners are instructed counsel and expert witnesses, as well as the primary relationship between solicitor and client. And, in the private client sector, a High Street conveyancing practice may well want to establish links with estate agents and mortgage lenders.

Such a scenario also has a spin-off benefit in that if the technologies being deployed – what this book calls the legistics – are of genuine benefit to all the parties, they can provide a way of cementing a closer and more permanent relationship between the client and the lawyer.

In other words if the service offered is just so damn useful and convenient that the client comes to rely on it, (an interactive case management link between a law firm's debt collection department and the client's credit management division is one area where this approach has already been applied) then the firm will have a competitive edge over any other lawyers pitching for the business – and the client will be less inclined to want to move the business anyway. (This is another manifestation of our old friend the 'virtuous circle'.)

A variation on this approach (same principle, different technology, but which so far I have only heard of being used by lawyers in the United States) is to supply important commercial clients with a video conference link, such as a videophone. Partly this is a goodwill/good PR gesture, but it is also a tacit recognition that clients' time is valuable and so, for convenience, here is a device that can put them in touch with their lawyers from the comfort of their own offices.

Anecdotal evidence suggests that some lawyers have actually seen an increase in business from these clients. The explanation seems to be that the video link is so convenient. It means a face-to-face conference is just a phone call away, whereas previously the client was more likely to delay consulting a lawyer because of the general hassle of arranging and attending meetings.

In an age when traditional client loyalties are waning, the clear lesson here is that the technology that digitally links the client to the lawyer may also prove to be the tie that binds the client far more closely to the lawyer.

New directions

So far we have been looking at digital technologies and their impact upon the more conventional approaches to legal practice – as a way of reinforcing the otherwise increasingly tenuous lawyer/client relationship; as a way for lawyers undertaking commoditised case management-style work to provide an enhanced service that both differentiates them from the competition and adds extra value for the client; and as a way of streamlining and automating the more routine aspects of client communications, freeing lawyers from endless interruptions so that they can concentrate on higher billing value added legal work. However, there is also a potentially new avenue opening up for legal services work in which lawyers utilise technology to become legal information providers.

Although lawyers – both solicitors and barristers – may deny it, there is a repetitive element to much of their legal work. Client 'A' wants a director's service contract or a franchise agreement drafting and so, at some time, will clients 'B', 'C' and 'D'. Having crafted a water-tight document for Client 'A', in 99 cases out of a 100, this will also serve as the boilerplate precedent for other clients.

From the lawyer's perspective this is an attractive option as a 'write once, resell many times' legal product. And, whereas commoditised case management work tends to be high volume, low profit margin work, with standard-form precedents you are moving into the realms of medium volume, high margin work that maximises the return from the lawyer's initial input of legal skills. (The traditional approach to case management work also usually requires a significant investment in IT systems before its potential can be fully realised, thus placing further pressure on profit margins, whereas this is not a prerequisite condition of precedents work.)

A number of law firms (although the same principles could also be adopted by members of the Bar) are now investigating the use of technology to have several more bites out of the legal value added cherry. For example, by selling precedents or similarly pre-packaged segments of legal information via the world wide web, the practice has the potential to reach a far wider catchment area than by normal promotional means.

Remember, the Internet is a shop window on the world that is open and accessible 24 hours a day. Yet, at the same time, the actual business side of the transaction can be streamlined to avoid the delays, inefficiencies and time consuming procedural rigmarole normally associated with this type of work.

Just consider which of these is the more attractive approach?

Client 'B' telephones to make an appointment and then physically visits the lawyer for a meeting. The lawyer then confirms the instructions and terms of business by post, before preparing and dispatching a draft of the document (which we know is a just another version of the Client 'A' precedent) to the client. Then, once this has been approved, the lawyer sends a copy of the final draft plus a bill for services rendered and, finally, sits back to wait for payment.

Alternatively, the client logs on to the law firm's web site at midnight, locates the precedent he wants, pays for it via a secure real-time credit card transaction, downloads the document onto his own computer system so he can produce copies via his own wordprocessing system, and then logs off again at approximately one minute past midnight.

The choice is a no-brainer – the client still gets the service he wants and the lawyer still gets paid (and paid a lot quicker) but neither side is forced to follow the rigid choreography of nineteenth century legal pedantry.

The good news is that a number of UK law firms located at both ends of the legal market spectrum are already putting these concepts into practice.

Linklaters and Clifford Chance, two of the biggest firms in the country, run what they call, respectively, their 'Blue Flag' and 'NextLaw' web sites. In effect these are extranets containing prepackaged information about the corporate, banking and financial regulatory regimes in different European and international legal jurisdictions.

This is very much the type of information on which the inhouse legal departments (see page 79) of larger commercial clients would normally consult their legal advisors but with these sites – subject to having an access password and agreeing to pay the appropriate fees, rumoured to be about £100,000 a year for the full 'Blue Flag' service – the same information is available instantly at the click (or two) of a mouse button.

Linklaters has been running its service since 1996 and is now, after taking into account both the IT and value added legal resources needed to create the site – over nine million words and 10,000 screen pages of material – breaking even on the project. 'NextLaw' is expected to become a commercially viable profit centre over the next five years.(Linklaters won the 'Innovation Award' for 'Blue Flag' in the 1998 *Lawyer*/HIFALs.)

Meanwhile, at the opposite end of the scale, a small north London software house, an offshoot of solicitors Landau & Cohen (what is it about north London and its legal IT entrepreneurs?), is now running an Internet-based legal precedents service called 'DirectLaw'. This allows members of the public to pay by credit card and then download legal documents – such as draft terms of service agreements for company directors – which they can then integrate with wordprocessing software and use for their own purposes.

The bad news – at least from the point of view of lawyers – is that there is currently also much other useful downloadable legal advice and information available on the web. Unfortunately the barristers and solicitors publishing it onto the web seem to have gripped the wrong end of the 'latent legal market' stick and are giving far too much of it away free of charge.

This is folly. These lawyers are giving away their own practice crown jewels. If the material has any value then it is worth charging people for it unless, for some aberrant reason, you have an aversion to making a profit. Besides, it is also a well documented phenomenon in online markets that once you have commenced a 'free' information service, it is then very difficult to convert it into a 'pay' business.

Leaving aside those people who do not currently use the services of lawyers and who are never likely to do so, many lawyers are still failing to grasp that what clients really want from digital technologies, such as the Internet, is not just information but also the added convenience of the delivery mechanism – and they are prepared to pay for it.

In the age of the Martini generation, there are enough people to recognise the benefits of legal services that can be delivered 'any time, any place, anywhere' to allow all digitally-aware lawyers to enjoy a decent standard of living and a healthier quality of life. True, 'the law may not exist to keep lawyers in business' but they still fulfil a vital role in any modern civilised society. That is why the digital communications revolution we are now living through is so important, because the technologies it is unleashing are set to play a key – if not crucial – part in keeping lawyers in the legal business.

Chapter Nine

A STRATEGY FOR LEGAL PRACTICE IN THE DIGITAL AGE

"Prosperity is ephemeral; because if a man behaves with patience and circumspection and the time and circumstances are such that this method is called for, he will prosper; but if time and circumstances change he will be ruined because he does not change his policy."
NICCOLO MACHIAVELLI – THE PRINCE

So where should legal practices, which are determined to survive and thrive into the twenty-first century, start when it comes to implementing client-facing technology systems?

The following eight point guide contains recommendations and actions lists intended to be of assistance to lawyers belonging to practices that may not be large enough to have their own inhouse IT departments or IT directors, (the ones that do are big and wealthy enough to be able to look after themselves) but at the same time do not fall into the category of those smaller 'Waiting for Godot' firms and chambers that will never themselves take the initiative to move into the digital age.

Recommendation One – Start now

While it may be true that technologies such as the Internet are only just starting to trickle down from being the preserve of enthusiasts and business users into the broader consumer market, that is no reason to procrastinate.

Consider it as dipping your toe into the digital waters to test the temperature. If you start running pilot projects now, you have time to hone your skills, build up your expertise – and even make a few mistakes – while there are still relatively few prospects around. This means that when the market does take off – as it will – you will be familiar with the technologies, know what to expect and thus be much better placed to take advantage of it than competitors who only wake up to the opportunities at a much later stage.

For example, if you are considering setting up a web site, by starting now you have a better chance of securing a good domain name for your site – and obviously more time in which to promote it. Leave it a couple of more years and you may only be able to register a less attractive name. By starting now you are also giving yourself more time in which to perfect your WWW pages, as even if you use an external consultancy you are unlikely to get the design as effective as you might like first time around.

Perhaps more importantly, by starting now you are also giving yourself an adequate opportunity to begin 'rolling out' these technologies to your colleagues and everyone else within the firm, so that they too understand what is going on. All your efforts as a digital age 'evangelist' will be negated if you are the only digitally aware lawyer among a practice populated by what amounts to an IT illiterate, computer phobic and technologically challenged underclass.

Recommendation Two – Budget to spend time

Most lawyers have spent between five and six years of their lives studying and training to practice law. Rather than see it all going to waste, it surely makes sense to invest some more time to ensure your practice survives.

If you want to stay in the legal business, you must be prepared to devote time to researching and investigating the opportunities that are being opened up by the digital communications revolution and legistics technologies.

Visit exhibitions and seminars, read books and magazines, surf the web to see what other lawyers are doing and set aside some 'blue sky gazing' time to think about what it is you are trying to achieve and where you want to go.

Recommendation Three – Budget to spend money

Budget to spend money on these projects. If you ask any external supplier (software house, legal publisher, stationery supplier) they will all confirm the view that lawyers are notorious for being unwilling to part with their money and reinvest it in the business. The net result is that many law firms and barristers' chambers are appallingly under-resourced and have to limp along with technologies that should have been replaced years (in some instances decades) ago.

It is noticeable that one of the key features differentiating the practices that are stagnating from the ones that are going places is their respective levels of investment in technology and related support services. You have got to speculate to accumulate and if you are not prepared to invest in your future, you cannot expect to have a future as a lawyer.

Having said that, with a little shopping around (which is also another reason to start now rather than leave it until you find yourself in a sellers' market) you should find that many technologies are actually a lot less expensive than you might first think.

For example you could spend tens of thousands of pounds on establishing a web site. Or you could register an Internet domain name with an Internet service provider (ISP) and set up a site with that ISP, including disk space on the ISP's server (this basically means they have all the hardware and connections to the Internet and you use them as a bureau) for as little as £400.

Similarly, the cost of installing an ISDN line – essential if you are considering video conferencing – has plummeted in recent months and, thanks to additional features such as 'multiple subscriber numbers', you can actually run data, Internet connections, fax, video conferencing and conventional voice calls across the same line so you may even be able to cut back on some of the other phone lines coming into the office.

Recommendation Four – Devise a practice development strategy
With some of the time you have set aside to consider your digital future, put some serious thought into preparing a development strategy for your practice.

Subject your work to a SWOT analysis – what are the strengths, weaknesses, opportunities and threats you face?

Where are you actually making money at the moment and where do you hope to be making it in the future?

What do your clients really think of the service they get and in what ways could you improve the way in which you deliver legal services to them?

Incidentally, do not ask them straight out if they are happy with your level of service, as out of politeness they will probably give you the answer they think you want to hear. Instead, sound them out on an informal basis to ascertain if there are any causes for concern, bottlenecks to overcome or enhancements that could be offered to make life easier for them.

A roundabout way of discovering this is to find out what your clients are having to do to meet the demands made by their customers. For example if you notice all your main commercial clients (or, in the case of barristers, their instructing solicitors) now have email addresses printed on their stationery, ask them if they would prefer to deal with you by email. (The same considerations also apply if your research reveals they are using video conferencing technology. If your clients are IT companies they will almost certainly have this technology.)

If you have international clients, you should certainly have an email facility and a web site containing latest practice information, so communications are no longer restricted to UK time zone office hours.

And, don't just stop with clients. Talk to your regular business 'partners' and associates, such as estate agents, insurance companies, local authorities, mortgage lenders and banks. If they have email services and web sites, they may also be interested in creating electronic links between your offices and themselves.

Recommendation Five – Begin laying the IT infrastructure

Start laying the groundwork now for your practice's digital future. For example, if you are having the office rewired or installing new phone lines, put in ISDN and give yourself the infrastructure upon which to build.

If you are considering replacing your existing computer systems (as are many businesses in order to avoid potential Year 2000 compliancy problems) ensure that your chosen supplier will be able to support interactive web-enabled technologies. You may not need them now, but you do not want to discover in, say, 18 months' time that your brand new case management software cannot provide an extranet link to a major commercial client, thus presenting you with a 'rock and a hard place' choice of either replacing the nearly-new system or risking losing the client.

There are already several 'general business' and at least a couple of more legal market specific 'stand alone' applications available in the UK that can support e-commerce activities, such as offering clients a will drafting facility that they can pay for online by credit card.

There are also a growing number of mainstream legal systems suppliers offering web-enabled 'integrated' products so that, for instance, the progress monitoring side of a case management system can produce reports that can be accessed both from within the law firm and from outside by a client accessing the information via a web browser/extranet link.

The key message here is that you may not need these digital technologies now, but you do not want to close off that avenue of opportunity for future use.

(On a practical note, do check what exactly your IT supplier is purporting to offer. Some may claim to have Internet divisions, but in fact all they want to do is sell you more hardware that you can probably live without, or web site design services you certainly should live without. Remember, most IT suppliers are primarily interested in what you buying their systems will do for them, not what their systems can do for you and your clients.)

Recommendation Six – six essential technologies to invest in

Most lawyers today should seriously consider investing in one or more of a total of six essential (and in some instances over-lapping) technologies if they want to plug into the digital communications revolution and be able to deliver truly client-facing legistical solutions. The six are:

(i) Telephony systems – It should be self evident that without telecoms links you cannot have electronic mail or access to the Internet, but many lawyers should also bear in mind that they could substantially improve the quality of service they provide to clients merely by investing in better conventional telephone systems.

With so many complaints being made about poor lawyer/client communications, is the traditional approach of the receptionist taking a note of incoming calls really the best way to handle telephone messages?

Are the messages getting through? Have you enough lines to handle incoming call traffic? (One set of barristers' chambers in the Temple reckons they were missing out on as many as three murder cases a week before they installed extra lines.) What happens when lawyers are out of the office and out of contact, for example when they are in court? Should you consider mobile phones, electronic pagers or call diversion services?

And, while it is very nice to have a receptionist answering the phones for 40 hours a week, what happens if a client wants to get in touch with you at any point during the remaining 128 hours of the week? We often hear about the long hours lawyers have to work – but many clients also work long hours or may be unable to make contact during conventional UK office hours.

Consider voice mail systems. Consider audio conferencing systems. Consider installing direct lines for each fee earner. Consider telephone answering services. Consider having fax machines at home. Or even just install a decent answering machine.

Why? Because these are simple and cheap solutions that can help a client feel they have not been abandoned by their legal advisers during the long hours between 5.00pm on a Friday evening and 9.30am on a Monday morning.

(ii) Electronic mail – Email is a seriously undervalued communications medium that is cheap, easy to use, convenient, saves time and is virtually instant. It is now very widely used within business and – as mentioned earlier – it also has a growing user base among consumers.

Or, to put it another way: if your commercial and private clients are using this medium, shouldn't you also be in the loop? (On a personal note, over the last 12 months I have noticed a considerable shift in the balance of message types coming into my own office. On an average day I now receive more email messages than the total number of phone calls and fax messages combined.)

Unlike the telephone, email also has the advantage of allowing you to reply at your own convenience – so no more awkward phone calls to interrupt your train of thought on another matter, or having to take calls at inconvenient times of the day or night to accommodate clients in different time zones.

There is a good argument for saying that email is the nearest thing the legal world has to a killer app, because it is both useful for clients and makes life easier for lawyers. Certainly it should be very highly placed on any legal IT shopping list.

(iii) Electronic document exchange systems – This is actually a rather grandiose name for a technology I suspect most lawyers already own, namely a wordprocessing system. The problem is most lawyers only ever see wordprocessing in terms of being a bigger and better typewriter.

Undoubtedly this is true but the technology allows you to do so much more than just create slick-looking documents which you then print onto sheets of paper, stick in an envelope, stamp and post off to the client to arrive hopefully the next working day.

Along with transmitting it almost instantaneously by fax, you can send it as an 'attached file' to an email message. You can 'copy' it on to a floppy disk and send it by post or courier. And, if you are dealing with a very large amount of documents, you could have them all put onto a CD-Rom to create an electronic or virtual case file – this last option does not even require the purchase of any additional technology as in most areas of the UK there are now companies who will offer this service on a bureau basis.

As you will know from your own use of wordprocessors,

it is very convenient to have documents in an electronic format as its makes their revision, amendment and redrafting that much simpler. If you look at this issue from the (commercial) client's perspective, exactly the same considerations apply – they too will almost inevitably find it convenient to have (or at least appreciate the offer of being supplied with) documents in a reworkable, interactive electronic format rather than just on paper.

A case of think not what your technology can do for you, but what your technology can do for your clients.

(iv) Direct information access systems – Just as clients may find it useful to have documents available in an electronic format as well as on paper, so they may also appreciate having access to information about the current status of projects you are undertaking on their behalf in a format other than paper.

In some instances it may be appropriate to give them direct access to parts of your own computer system – some case management software offers this facility. In other cases you may 'publish' the information onto a secure part of the Internet (or an extranet) to which only they have access – again there are third-party software applications that can provide this information. It may even be appropriate to download the information into a spreadsheet and either send it to them on a floppy disk or as an email attachment.

The specific mechanism does not actually matter. What is important is that if clients do have the need for direct electronic access to certain types of information, the technology now exists to deliver it to them.

Clients know this and you should know this and now be investing in the appropriate technology. Above all, there is no longer any excuse for continuing to send them this type of material in a traditional paper format only.

Some lawyers are getting very upset about direct access

and regard it as a demand too far by pushy clients. However, if you look at it in a more positive light, it is actually yet another technology with the potential to make life easier for lawyers. After all, instead of the inconvenience of you being at the beck-and-call of a client and having to break from your (hopefully) value added work to prepare a progress report according to their agenda, that client can find out the information for themselves at their own convenience – it is the Martini factor at work again.

(v) Web sites – With only 400 law firms in the UK on the web, there is still room to make a splash and a practice (or chambers) web site is one of the clearest ways there is of marking your territory and saying, "Here we are, we are a modern technologically clued up bunch of lawyers who are prepared to move with the times rather dwell on the past". (See also 'Twelve Tips' in the Legal Technology Lexicon below.)

As well as its promotional value as a statement of intent, a web site also provides the foundations for delivering interactive legal services to clients.

It can be used as a public or, via password protected areas, a private source of legal information to clients and prospective clients. It can be a communications medium, with clients submitting instructions in one direction and lawyers delivering legal services in the other direction. It can be linked to accounts and case management systems to provide varying degrees of direct access.

And, once again, it is a technology that allows the client to work to their own agenda while at the same time freeing the lawyer to keep to his or her own agenda.

(vi) Video conferencing – Despite having the appearance of being one of the more exotic manifestations of the digital communications revolution, video conferencing systems offer one of the more obvious and immediate benefits: you can hold a face-to-face meeting without compelling one or more of the parties to take time out of their busy day to travel to a meeting.

Lawyers like the concept, clients like the concept and the courts and legal institutions also like the concept. Mention has already been made of the benefits in terms of cost savings and freeing lawyers to concentrate on better paying value added work. Once again there is also a potential benefit in terms of improving the lawyer's quality of life.

For example, there is the firm in the north of England that has installed a video conferencing system to link the fee earners in the practice's four branch offices. As well as avoiding the need for the firm's own staff to travel between the separate offices for meetings, this facility also means clients can visit the office most convenient for them and still have a 'face-to-face' conference, via the video link, with a particular legal adviser.

From the clients' point of view, as long as they get the lawyer they want and can have 'virtual' meetings without the inconvenience of lengthy journeys, it does not really matter to them whether the lawyer is located 100 yards away, 100 miles away – or even in another country.

Recognising this, the firm's senior partner has now installed a video conference link at his holiday villa in Provence. The client still sees a lawyer in a business suit sitting at a desk in front of a book-lined wall. But, what the client does not see is that beneath the desk the senior partner is wearing a pair of trunks and that the book-lined wall is actually part of a room that opens onto a swimming pool! This is a true story – the firm's identity is not disclosed for obvious reasons.

And why shouldn't lawyers take advantage of technologies that can help mix business with pleasure?

Recommendation Seven – Start to think digital
For lawyers moving from the postage stamps and fountains pens

era to the age of virtually instant global online communications, it is essential to change your mind-set and start to think digital.

For example, there are currently many law firms in the UK which may have email facilities but have not yet entered into the email culture of using it properly. Incoming messages are never acknowledged or if they are, it is by a telephone call or letter which can be irksome as the reason the sender probably sent the email message in the first place was because he didn't want to speak to his lawyer or was hoping for a quick response.

Similarly there are firms that would appear never to check their email in boxes on a regular basis. On some occasions I have known weeks to elapse before I have received a response. You would never dream of letting your telephone ring, unanswered, for days at a time, so why do it with email? Better not to have the technology at all than to have it, raise client expectations and then misuse it.

Still on the subject of email culture, ensure it (and your own site address if you have one) appears on all your stationery, business cards, promotional literature and any advertising (recruitment or otherwise) that you may run. And make sure your staff also know it – and know it properly – so they can give it out to callers. Once again, this is a failing I have frequently encountered within law firms.

Thinking digital also means applying a new approach to other activities, such as marketing.

For example, law firms are often invited to sponsor local events or charity fund-raising campaigns. As a tactic there is nothing wrong with law firms being involved in this, not least because it helps promote lawyers in a positive light. But, instead of paying for a tombstone advertisement in a souvenir programme or brochure that no one will ever open again, think creatively. Perhaps sponsor the charity's web site or even give them some space on your site.

With a growing number of chambers of commerce, small business associations and local authorities also using the web as a promotional medium, why not consider links with their sites? If you handle legal aid work, you might consider talking to your local cybercafe (if there is one) as some of their customers – particularly male adolescents – could overlap with your client base.

And, remember, not all you clients may be as switched on as you. A number of firms and sets of chambers have discovered that providing their prospective clients with an opportunity to 'surf the Internet', or take part in a live video conference, can provide a novel, yet at the same time useful, angle to an otherwise conventional promotional event.

Recommendation Eight – Keep watching for new developments

Finally, avoid the short-termism that has dogged so many previous law office automation exercises. With digital technology you cannot afford to make your selection, install the new system – and then sit back and do nothing for another five or ten years until you feel it is time buy a replacement system.

To paraphrase Machiavelli, just because a particular approach to the business of law, or application of a certain technology works in one set of circumstances, does not mean it will always work. As circumstances change over time, so must the business methods and technologies being deployed.

The speed at which the digital age is progressing means technologies, such as extranets, that were almost unheard of a couple of years ago are now becoming mainstream, while the impact and potential of more novel technologies, such as interactive digital television, can today only be imagined. But they too will be mainstream before the decade is out.

For example, the next generation of 'Office' suites, such as Corel Office 9.0, Lotus SmartSuite Millennium and Microsoft Office 2000 will all include features to make it easier to create documents for use in both conventional paper formats and web-enabled electronic formats for publishing on the Internet and on intranets.

Similarly, the price of video conferencing systems is falling to a point where they are becoming a realistic option for small businesses. And speech recognition systems are improving with each new version, so that sooner – rather than later – they will become a viable technology. (My own personal view is that the day to buy speech recognition is the day Microsoft gives the technology its official blessing by incorporating it into products such as Windows or Word.)

On a more mundane day-to-day level, computer-using lawyers also need to monitor changes to ensure their existing IT systems do not become too dated and consequently incompatible with the systems being used by their clients. For instance, at the time of writing, there is a move towards what are called '32-bit' software applications. These will run on Windows 95/NT/98 operating systems but not PCs using the earlier '16-bit' Windows 3.1 operating system.

Or, to take another example, WordPerfect Version 6.1 will allow you to exchange data files with both other WordPerfect 6.1 users and users of the earlier WordPerfect 5.1 program. But, hard luck if you need to communicate with someone using WordPerfect Version 8, as that is an incompatible product. On the other hand, if you were to upgrade to Version 8.0 then not only would you be able to communicate with users of earlier WordPerfect products, but you could even exchange files with, say, clients running the rival Microsoft Word 97 product.

Compatibility is a one-way street. Later products can co-exist with earlier products, but earlier products cannot 'talk' to later products. To avoid finding yourself stranded up the IT equivalent of an evolutionary cul-de-sac and unable to exchange files with clients, expert witnesses or even court officials, it is essential to keep upgrading your technology.

So, keep watching for new developments. Keep attending exhibitions and seminars. Keep reading the literature: books, newspapers and magazines. Keep surfing the web to see what the competition are doing. And, above all, keep in touch with your clients to ensure you continue (ideally) to anticipate and address their changing needs, for in the final analysis the clients are the only people who really matter in today's legal business.

Legal Technology Lexicon

Administrative tail – the ratio of fee earners (lawyers) to support staff (secretaries and clerical staff) within a legal practice. One of the objectives of any law office automation project should be to maximise the number of lawyers that can be supported by the minimum number of support staff.

Authoring tools – software packages to simplify the process of designing web pages and converting existing documents created on wordprocessors into HTML files. Microsoft FrontPage and Adobe PageMill are two of the most widely used applications.

Bandwidth – a measurement of the capacity of the Internet and other networks to carry data. Simple text messages, such as email, take up very little bandwidth whereas video conferencing needs a lot, which is why you cannot use a normal phone line for video conferencing. The bandwidth issue also crops up when you are surfing the web. The worst time is in the evening when the Internet is being widely accessed in the USA as well as in the UK. The best time (for UK users) is early morning.

Barbican (Solex or the Solicitors and Legal Office Exhibition) – currently the UK's leading legal technology exhibition. Held every June in London, it is the venue for most law office systems' new product launches. 'Legal Tech New York' is the equivalent US event. Always worth visiting and admission is free.

Blue Flag – the Linklaters' extranet site providing 'commoditised' legal information for larger commercial clients. Although this is a novel use of interactive web technology, it is worth bearing in mind that it is designed primarily for clients with their own inhouse legal advisers – as distinct from lay members of the public. And it is a commercial venture – not a charity – intended to make a profit for the partners at Linklaters.

Brochureware – typical first generation law firm web sites containing little more than an online copy of the firm's conventional promotional brochure. To be avoided if your senior partner's ego will allow it.

Browser software – the graphical user interface program for accessing the web. At the time of writing the two most widely used browser products are Microsoft Internet Explorer 3.0 and Netscape Navigator 3.0 – both are now available free of charge.

Bytes – a unit for measuring data. Eight 'bits' make one byte. One kilobyte (1Kb or just 1K) contains 1024 bytes – a sheet of A4 text takes up about 4Kb. One megabyte (1Mb) contains 1024K. Use in the context of "my PC has 64Mb (pronounced "meg") of RAM memory".

CD-Rom (compact disks) – a generic term for a convenient and high volume storage medium that can hold the equivalent of several dozen floppy disks full of data. In the legal world its two main uses are: as an interactive publishing platform as many law books are now published on CD complete with highly sophisticated indexing and search software and as a means of creating electronic case files – for example instead of the two sides in litigation having to exchange large volumes of copies of paper documents, the originals can be scanned, stored and subsequently accessed on CD-Rom.

Case management system (also called **fee earner support systems and case management lite products**) – one of the more widely used legal software applications in solicitors' offices. Used to its best effect when processing large volumes of similar type work, such as 'bent bumper' motor insurance claims or debt collection. Many of the more modern systems now incorporate varying degrees of client facing technology.

Cookies – mini software programs used by some web sites to monitor and keep track of visitors. The catch is that the web site loads them on to the visitor's PC. A lot of controversy surrounds the use of cookies, not least because there are rumours they are now being used by hackers. If you are building a web site, do not include them because users do not like them. If you are a user and you encounter one, just say no – all modern browsers give you the option to refuse to accept cookies.

Cyberspace (also known as the **Information Superhighway**) – much hyped phrase used to describe the electronic or virtual environment in which Internet users operate. Now largely exists in the minds of thriller writers and heading towards kitsch corner. If you want to be taken seriously, do not call yourself a 'cyber lawyer'.

Dial up services – the most commonly encountered basis for communications between home or small businesses and the Internet via an ISP. Access is by personal computer and modem via a conventional telephone line.

Digital technology – portmanteau phrase used to describe IT and communications systems that employ discrete binary codes. What is important about this stuff is that it makes life so much easier for users to exchange information between different types of device – for example you can now surf the web with a mobile phone.

Digiterati – the techies, enthusiasts and early adopters of Internet technology who were prepared to build up the skills necessary to master the medium.

Domain name – the part of an Internet address that specifies your business name and location, so other computers can locate your web site or send you email messages. Most law firms have a '.com' or '.co.uk' suffix to their domain names, as in 'ourfirm.com'. Do try to register a simple domain name that is not littered with underscores or tildes as in 'our~law_firm.com' as this makes them less than memorable.

Document management system – a widely used software application in larger law firms designed to index, archive and retrieve all the thousands of documents being produced on wordprocessors. The latest version can also handle documents stored on web sites and internal intranets.

E-Commerce (or **e-business**) – the use of the Internet and related technologies as an interactive transactional medium for buying and selling products and services – as distinct from merely promoting them but still distributing them through conventional channels.

Electronic mail (or **email**) – a primarily text based medium that is rapidly competing with fax and the telephone as a method of communication. Email can be both an internal service on a network or intranet, external via the Internet, or web-based via the email facilities included in most web browser software.

Email address – this has three elements: the recipient's identity, an "@" sign and the domain name, as in 'johnbrown@ourfirm.com'. For some unknown reason, legal secretaries are frequently unwilling to disclose email addresses to the outside world.

Encryption – a technology used to code and decode electronic communications so that if confidential material does inadvertently fall into the wrong hands, its contents remain secure because they do not have the 'key' to decrypt it. Legal uncertainties have delayed its adoption on a global basis, but it now looks set to become the way business or legal critical documents are exchanged electronically.

Evangelism – as in 'software evangelist' or 'Internet evangelist'. Sharing your enthusiasm for a new technology with the marketplace (in this case lawyers) so that they can see the business benefits for themselves and feel inspired to use them.

Extranets (sometimes **Xtranets**) – an intranet whose membership has been extended to include users on a select number of outside third party networks, typically those belonging to clients, to create a trading or information sharing community. Security technology – such as 'firewall' systems – is used to maintain the privacy of extranets and prevent access from the wider public Internet.

FTP (file transfer protocol) – a simple-to-use mechanism for uploading and downloading files to and from the Internet. If you have a web site stored on an ISP's server, you will use FTP to place and remove HTML pages. This is really under-the-bonnet stuff you don't need to worry about.

Firewalls – security technology that sits between your internal computer network and the external Internet to prevent hacking or other forms of unauthorised access. Relevant if you have your own servers but irrelevant if you have an ISP as they will have their own firewalls. Increasingly these systems also have facilities to restrict outgoing access to the Internet, so a firm can prevent its staff from visiting a sport or porn web site.

GIF (graphic interchange format) – the most frequently encountered file format for graphics images that are used on web sites. Only three rules apply: do you really need them? If you do, keep them small. And, always supply a text alternative so people browsing with the 'load images' menu option turned off can see what they are missing. "Oh, it is a 200K picture of the firm's senior partner. ZZzzz"

GSM – global system for mobile communications. Most of the latest digital mobile phones follow the GSM standard. It means you can link into the cell phone network even when you are in another country. You can also use your mobile phone in conjunction with a laptop computer to access the Internet.

GUI (graphical user interface) – all modern computer operating systems, such as Microsoft Windows, and software applications, such as web browsers, have a GUI front end. Pronounced "gooey", their great benefit is that they are easy to use to the point of being intuitive. All GUIs use the WIMP approach.

Hackers – near legendary creatures now encountered more in fiction than real life. They do exist but are primarily interested in breaching the security of (hacking into) e-commerce sites to get hold of credit card data, disrupting party political sites – there is a strong anarchist trend among hackers – or breaking into US military sites to see who really did land at Roswell or to try to start Word War III.

Hits – a measure of the number of people visiting a web site. Market researchers now use more sophisticated methods because the inherent problem with counting hits is you never know if 100 people have visited your site once, or one person has visited your site 100 times.

Home page – this is the first page you see by default when you visit a web site. Sometimes called the welcome page and will usually have the word 'welcome' in its URL.

HTML – the programming language of the web. Unlike most computer languages, this is very simple to use and thus making it commercially viable for law firms to develop complex web sites. (For example the HTML code necessary to create the sentence "These words are printed in bold and italic text," would be "These words are printed in <B>bold</B> and <I>italic</I> text".) An alternative approach is to use a web authoring tool which hides the 'raw' HTML code. All HTML files have either an .htm, or .html suffix.

Hypertext Links (or **hyperlinks**) – a standard cross-referencing system that allows items of information on one web page to be linked to information on the same page, on the same web site or even on a web site belonging to an organisation on the other side of the globe. Hyperlinks provide a simple to use and almost instant mechanism for navigating around the millions of pages of information now stored on intranets and the Internet. On most web pages, words containing a hypertext link are underlined and displayed in a different colour to the surrounding wording.

Interactive – any system allowing two way communications between the sender and receiver. The most basic form of interactive web site is one that allows the visitor to send the site operator an email message.

Iterations – upgrades to software are typically given version numbers. Thus WordPerfect 8.0 follows WordPerfect 7.0. In addition there will usually be a number of minor upgrades between the release of major upgrades – thus Internet Explorer 3.1 follows Internet Explorer version 3.0. As a rule of thumb always go for the later iterations (ie 3.1) as these inevitably include 'patches' and bug fixes to overcome problems found in preceding versions. With other software – such as Windows 95 – the bug fixes will be found in the 'service packs' that are produced at a later date. It is the difference between being leading edge and bleeding edge.

Internet (or **the Net**) – a publicly accessible service comprising four main areas: the world wide web (or WWW), email, the FTP file transfer system and the newsgroups discussion groups/bulletin board areas.

Internet service providers (ISPs) – in effect bureaux providing access to the Internet, web site hosting and related services. Unless you are with a large law firm that has its own direct access to the Internet, you will probably use an ISP. There are now several hundred of these operating in the UK, so either shop around for a good deal or choose on personal recommendation. Most ISPs should be able to offer access at local call rates.

Intranets – a private subset of the Internet, typically restricted to users of an internal network. Intranets frequently make use of browser software, but an alternative used by some law firms is to base intranets on Lotus Notes.

ISDN – integrated services digital network. After a slow start ISDN is becoming established as a global standard for high speed, high quality telephone communications, including video conferencing and Internet access.

Java – an interactive programming language for the Internet. Forget the hype, you can live without it.

Know-how systems – flavour of the month technology among larger law firms. It is intended to capture the benefits of a practice's accumulated legal expertise. Few know-how projects have so far moved beyond the pilot stage. However, they will typically be run across an intranet and make a lot of use of hyperlinks.

Killer apps (killer applications) – the Holy Grail of office automation, a software product or application that will simultaneously reduce overheads, increase productivity, boost efficiency, maximise profitability and generally transform the lives of users.

Kiosks – the theory is that one way to bring the law and other public services closer to the people is to create informal consumer-friendly information centres (they often look like 'Photo-Me' booths) located in public spaces, such as shopping malls, that offer passers-by online access, web browsing, video conference links and other forms of interactive electronic access to official sources of information. Note the word 'theory'. The London Borough of Lewisham spent two years and the better part of a quarter of million pounds on a network of twelve 'tellytalk' kiosks but, despite winning awards and being praised by politicians as 'the future of public services delivery', the project has been axed because it seems the public were not interested in using them.

LAN (local area network) – most basic form of computer network with different devices linked by cables.

Leased lines – a very high speed alternative to ISDN for larger organisations that need to be online for lengthy periods of time. Leased line services are usually described in terms of communications speed – eg kilostream, megastream – and are widely used by law firms wanting to establish communications links between computers in different offices.

Latent legal market – an 'urban myth' that suggests that if the law was made more user-friendly, with lots of legal information made freely available on the web, then people who are currently alienated by the legal process would make greater use of it. The jury is still out on this theory but either way it is not going to help lawyers make more money.

Lawyer/**HIFAL Awards** – annual awards organised by *The Lawyer* magazine. Generally regarded as the UK legal world's answer to the Oscars.

Legal Technology Insider **(LTi)** – a fortnightly subscription-only newsletter that has become essential reading for everyone in the UK (plus Ireland and parts of the Continent) who is seriously involved in the law office automation field. If you develop, sell, buy or use legal IT, you read the 'Insider'. It is available in both conventional and web-enabled formats.

Legistics – the use of advanced technologies, such as the Internet, to deliver legal advice and information services to clients and other lawyers.

LINK (Legal Electronic NetworK) – the most widely used lawyer-to-lawyer discussion forum and email service in the UK. It is free and well worth using, both as a way of easing yourself into the email culture and encountering like-minded lawyers prepared to swap technology advice, tips and experiences.

Litigation support systems – widely used technology in larger law firms used to manage the enormous volumes of documents now encountered in major litigation. A system will contain one or more of the following elements: scanners, optical character recognition systems, subjective and objective indexing systems, full text retrieval, and real-time transcription. Sometimes also called **DIP (document image processing)** or **EDM (electronic document management)** and frequently used in conjunction with CD-Rom technology.

Martini generation – The growing number of people, including law firm clients, who are familiar with and expect to be able to use email and interactive web sites as a way of accessing information and services. They know such facilities exist to make information available 'any time, any place, anywhere'.

Micropayments – secure online banking and payment mechanisms that will allow organisations to cost effectively sell information from their web sites by the page or document. Although not an online service, the MONDEX cashless system currently being trialed in parts of the UK is an example of a technology that will allow micropayments. An inherent problem with online credit card transactions, secure or otherwise, is that transaction charges make it an uneconomic mechanism for small sums of money.

Modem – a device that enables computers to talk to each other over a standard telephone line. Modem speeds are measured according to internationally agreed 'V' standards for 'baud rates'. For example a V.34 modem can transmit data at speeds (ie has a baud rate) of up to 28,800 bits per second (or 28.8 kbps). Modem speeds are getting progressively faster but the physical limitations on conventional phone lines mean they will never be as fast as the 128 kbps speed of ISDN.

Multimedia – any form of technology that can bring together different media, such as text, sound and moving video clips. Sounds gimmicky but in the right context – such as a courtroom presentation system where the different media can be combined to explain complex evidence – it can be useful. For the home user it means you can play Lara Croft's latest 'Tomb Raider' adventure game on your PC, with lots of moving images and noisy sound effects.

Netiquette – the etiquette of the Internet. An unwritten rule that you do not try to cram commercial services down newsgroup members throats by blatantly plugging your business. Legitimate comment about the legal implications of a story or thread is acceptable but not sending everyone a message saying 'Need a lawyer? Just call us'. See also 'spamming'.

Newsgroups (sometimes called **usenet groups, discussion forums, bulletin board services** or **BBS**) – one of the original parts of the Internet although now overshadowed by the web. Provides an interactive discussion area – there are about 30,000 different subject groups available globally – where users can post comments and requests for information and other users can respond to them as part of a 'thread'. There is actually a potential marketing opportunity here by adding legal comments, where relevant, to a discussion chain or thread. But, beware of 'netiquette'.

Personal Computer (PC) – the most commonly encountered piece of computer technology in homes and offices today. They can run by themselves in a stand-alone capacity or can be linked together as part of a network. The two basic formats are the desktop model and the portable laptop or notebook model. Most law firms and barristers' chambers have PCs running one of the versions of the Microsoft Windows operating system. This is now available in Windows 3x, 95, 98 and NT Workstation flavours.

Practice (or **Chambers**) **Management System (PMS)** – very widely used law office automation software. The earliest versions just handled accounts (and, in the case of solicitors, time recording) but the latest versions can also provide a lot of useful client, work type, financial and management information, so practice managers have an opportunity to analyse data and run their firms (or chambers) on a more commercial business footing.

Push technology – the traditional approach to web information was to publish it on a site and then wait for people to access it. Push technology aims to be proactive and send the relevant information to the user as soon as it becomes available – like Stock Market 'ticker' services – rather than waiting for them to find it. But as experience suggests that once the novelty has worn off, the user tends to turn these facilities off, these systems are probably best avoided. Email can also be used as a simple push mechanism.

Satellites – there are currently at least two major projects underway to create 'Internets in the sky' that will be able to deliver their services via a global network of low earth orbit communications satellites. However, as it is likely to be four to five years before these services are fully up and running, don't hold your breath waiting for them to come to a PC near you.

Set top boxes (or **STBs**) – most web access is currently via personal computers but the launch of digital television services in 1998, including British Interactive Broadcasting, will be based on set-top decoder boxes which will provide home users with entertainment, web access and interactive services via their television sets.

Society for Computers and Law (SCL) – a club for UK techie enthusiasts.

Spamming – electronic junk mail sent unsolicited to a large number of Internet users. There are discussions in the United States about making this practice illegal. Certainly spamming will not win you any friends and you can upset users sufficiently that they will bombard you back with junk mail or by returning multiple copies of your original message – this is known as 'flaming'.

Speech (or voice) recognition – technology that uses mathematical algorithms to convert sound waves into instructions a computer can understand. The two main uses are 'speech-to-text' – so you can 'dictate' directly into a wordprocessing document without using the computer keyboard; and 'command and control' which allows you to control a computer by spoken commands, such as "print", "save", "open file". One day every PC will have a microphone attached to it along with a mouse and a keyboard – but not just yet.

TLA – three letter acronyms. The computer industry makes such widespread use of them that they should be declared a notifiable disease.

Techie enthusiasts (or **anoraks, geeks or nerds**) – management consultants, IT specialists and lawyers who are so full of enthusiasm about the technical under-the-bonnet aspects of new technologies and gadgets that they neglect to mention the business benefits to ordinary mortals, who consequently only feel inspired to fall asleep. There again, Bill Gates of Microsoft had a reputation for being a nerd and it has helped make him one of the richest men on the planet – he is currently worth $51 billion.

Telecommuting (or **teleworking**) – the use of technology to create the 'virtual' office, so staff can be in contact with each other, as well as access and work on centrally held records and files from remote locations, including working from home. Laptops, the Internet, GSM, email and video conferencing all now make this approach technically feasible and it is only the human factor that has prevented it from being widely employed. (Solicitec, the sponsors of this book, are now making widespread use of telecommuting to create a virtual office environment within their own organisation.)

Twelve web site design tips. Whether you use an external agency to create your web site or tackle it inhouse there are twelve basic design features all legal sites should always take into account:

(i) Design for the real world. Most users do not have high speed ISDN links to the Internet, the newest versions of browser software, large VDU screens or the latest multimedia plug-ins, so adapt your designs accordingly.

(ii) Be sparing with graphics. Too many sites are cluttered with irrelevant image files that merely slow download times. In particular, pictures of solicitors are seldom a selling point on a web site. The rule of thumb is that if a page takes longer to download than you can hold your breath, most users will move on.

(iii) Is it relevant? So your site features Java and ActiveX, is accessed via an enormous 'image map' and makes extensive use of 'frames'. Big deal. But does it add anything to the greater sum of human knowledge or just show off your technical skills? If you do need to structure page content, try tables instead of frames.

(iv) Don't alienate the punter. Never design a site that is optimised to just one browser. Why alienate at least 50 percent of all prospective visitors? And don't offer visitors the opportunity to download a copy of your browser of choice – they won't, they've better things to do with their lives.

(v) Make life easy for visitors. It is only natural to want to get as much information as possible about site visitors, as they may be prospective clients, but don't slow things down by making them complete lengthy 'visitors books' (an annoying feature of a lot of newspaper sites) before they can access it.

(vi) Content is king. Web designers love elaborate design elements, which is fine if the web site is intended to promote a new rock group or a special effects-laden Hollywood movie. With legal sites, however, most visitors just want to see what you have to say, so focus on editorial content.

While I am a firm believer that legal web sites should be about trying to keep lawyers in business rather than rendering them redundant – and I would therefore advise against giving away large amounts of free legal information – it is nevertheless essential to provide some information to make the surfer's visit worthwhile. Give them a 'taster' that shows your skills and hopefully whets their appetites, so that eventually they do consult you on a professional basis.

For example, a commentary on a recent court case or new piece of legislation might be used to sow the seeds of the FUD (fear, uncertainty and doubt) factor and prompt prospective clients to think 'that could happen to us, we'd better ask a lawyer to review our current terms and conditions of business'. (This approach can obviously also be used by members of the Bar promoting their services to instructing solicitors.)

(vii) Think newspaper not brochureware And if content is king, make it easy to find by putting the material at the beginning rather than burying it deep within the site.

There is a tendency to see web sites as being along the same lines as conventional promotional material: glossy front page, followed by picture of senior partner or head of chambers, followed by picture of new office premises, followed by profiles of other lawyers, and so on with a 'what's new' section tagged on almost as an afterthought. (This is why some sites are dismissively termed 'brochureware'.) Wrong. Your model should be that of a newspaper with latest developments and contents list on the front page and 'softer' items on the inside.

(viii) A web site is not just for Christmas. If you want people to return to your site (and you should, as it is unlikely you will win new business from a first pass) keep it fresh by updating it on a regular basis so they have a reason to return – and tell them when the next update is scheduled.

(ix) Minimise outside links. Unless you are running a 'directory' style site, keep hyperlinks to third party pages to a minimum. It is hard enough to attract people to a site in the first place, so don't encourage them to go elsewhere.

(x) Provide email links. The simplest form of interactive web site is a basic 'mailto' facility so visitors can email you directly from the site while they are still browsing.

(xi) Provide contact details. On the other hand, in your enthusiasm for the digital communications revolution, do not overlook the fact that visitors may want to know your geographic location or to telephone, fax, DX or even write to you by mail, so also always provide full address details.

(xii) Do not use visitor counters – this is the digital age's equivalent of train spotting and is just so very, very sad.

Incidentally, the creation of a straightforward text plus simple graphics site is well within the capabilities of any half-way computer literate lawyer. There is no shortage of cheap and easy to follow 'Teach yourself HTML' type books. There are web authoring software programs, such as Microsoft FrontPage, and

HTML conversion facilities in wordprocessing packages to help do the job for you. And you can always find out how other firms have created a particular look, colour scheme or column layout to their sites by using the 'View Source' menu option on a web browser as this will reveal the underlying HTML code.

URL (uniform resource locator) – every page on the web has its own unique reference known as the URL. Most URLs start with the prefix 'http://www' followed by the domain name and page reference. Thus a home page might have the URL of 'http://www.ourfirm.com/welcome.htm'.

Video conferencing – a potentially very useful technology offering the simultaneous transmission of sound and moving images down an ISDN telephone line so you can see the person with whom you are talking. Variations on this technology also allow users to see documents and even work together on a joint software application, such as drafting a legal agreement. The technology comes in a number of formats including stand alone desktop videophones, big screen group conferencing systems and PC-based systems that display the video image in a corner of a computer VDU screen, while simultaneously allowing the parties to 'share' a software application so that, for example, they can work together on the final draft of a document. The cost (now falling substantially) plus the lack of a critical mass (not many people out there to video conference with) have unfortunately held back their take-up by lawyers.

WAN (wide area network) – the linking of LANS in two or more offices to create a single network. Increasingly WANs are used to carry an intranet.

Web enablement – the growing trend to build into software the ability to create documents in an alternative Internet compatible format, so it can be accessed by a web browser or posted onto the Internet. Currently one of the most widely used web-enabled applications is Microsoft Word 7.0. However, a number of legal systems suppliers are now building web enablement into their case and practice management systems.

WIMP – all GUI systems contain four elements: a screen divided into windows, the use of little pictograms called icons instead of text instructions, an on screen pointer and a handheld unit called a mouse for moving the pointer between icons.

Woolf Report – the 1996 report *Access to Justice* produced by Lord Woolf, the Master of the Rolls, is widely regarded as laying down a useful framework for reforming the civil justice system in England and Wales to make it faster, cheaper and more efficient. Among the 303 recommendations made are several relating to technology, including the use of video conferencing in routine hearings and the need for judges to have caseload management systems to allocate resources, schedule workloads and electronically diarise cases. As yet the thorny question of how these reforms will be funded has yet to be answered but, along with video conferencing, lawyers can expect to be making greater use of CD-Rom/litigation support systems and email links between the courts and the various parties involved in a case.

Wordprocessing (WP) – the most widely used software application in the legal world. The two main products are Microsoft Office and Corel WordPerfect and both now have facilities to allow users to 'save' documents as web pages.

Workflow (or **BPR, business process re-engineering**) – this is the theory that to get the best out of law office automation systems you need to change – or re-engineer – your internal working procedures so that tasks flow from one logical stage to another. It works in some law firms, it doesn't work in others and a lot of firms just never bother to try.

World Wide Web (**WWW** or **web**) – this is the graphical part of the Internet and currently consists of nearly 400 million 'pages' of information stored on millions of web sites around the world. The URL system and hypertext links mean that all of them can be accessed by a few 'clicks' of a mouse. It is the ultimate reference library for the digital age – unfortunately when too many people are online simultaneously you may think a more appropriate name is the 'world wide wait'.

Year 2000 (**Y2K** also known as **the Millennium computing bug**) – there is widespread concern that when December 31st 1999 becomes January 1st 2000, a very large number of the world's computers will suffer the electronic equivalent of a nervous breakdown because they will be unable to work out why 1999 has suddenly become the year 1900. The problem stems from the use of the 'double digit' date format in a lot of older computer technology and related programming. Thus 1998 is coded as just '98'. Lawyers should certainly ensure their systems are Y2K compliant but in addition you also need to check that your clients' systems are millennium proof. Wry amusement is probably not the emotion that will come to mind when, in early January 2000, you discover that although you can issue invoices, none of your clients will be capable of processing them for a further six months.

Zen (and the art of computing) – computers, software, the Internet and other forms of digital technology are inanimate objects and should function according to the logical rules of science. But sometimes they just don't and there may no apparent reason why your system 'freezes' or crashes one day but works perfectly well the next. Instead of getting annoyed or upset, console yourself with the thought that computers are such complex devices that instead of being surprised when sometimes they don't work, we should actually be amazed they ever work at all.

Acknowledgement

All trademarks, product and brand names are acknowledged and recognised as belonging to their respective owners. Unless otherwise stated, all material and sources of information are taken from the archives of *Legal Technology Insider*. The state of the law, legal profession and technology is accurate as at 1st September 1998.

The Quest for the killer app continues

In common with lawyers, legal systems house Solicitec is also in search of the 'killer app'.

Today the company is the largest supplier of Windows case management systems in the UK and one reason for Solicitec's success is its view of where both the suppliers and buyers of legal services are heading in the future.

In its latest release, Solicitec's SolCase 98 case management product incorporates many of the features of the client-facing legal desktop outlined in this book, including document imaging, document management, workflow technology and the ability to interface with advanced communications mediums, including the Internet and video conferencing.

However perhaps the main feature that makes SolCase 98 a potential killer app is the SolCase Online facility, a web-enablement tool that allows solicitors to give their clients access to their own cases via a secure and controlled Internet browser.

For further information or a demonstration of a real killer app, contact Solicitec on 0113 2262000 or visit http://www.solicitec.com